Big Apple Diaries

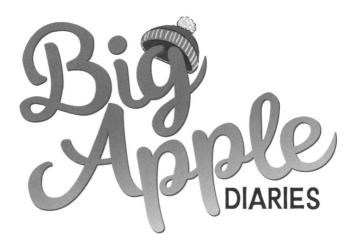

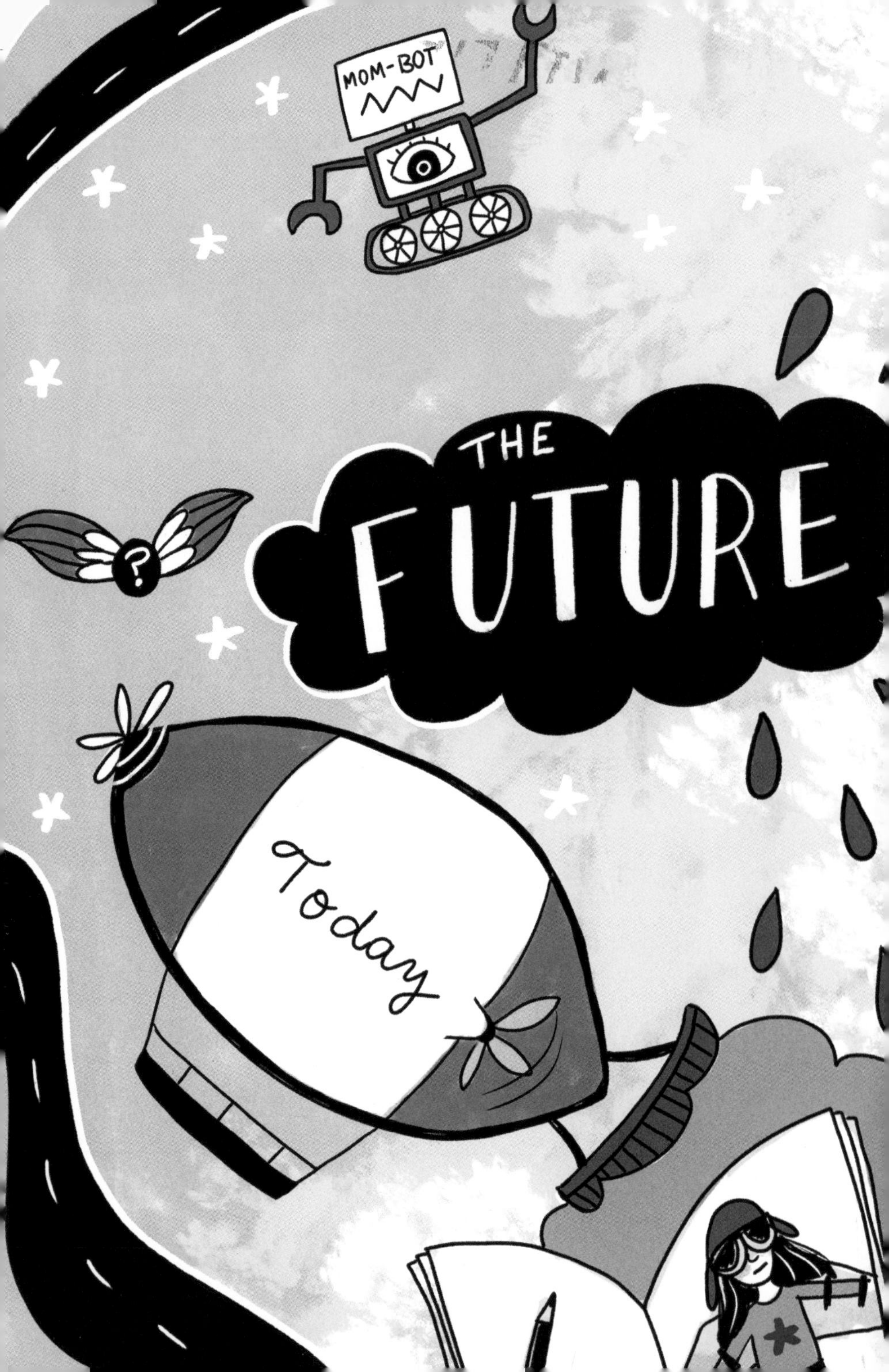
MOM-BOT
THE FUTURE
Today

3 1526 05532760 2

Big Apple
DIARIES

ALYSSA BERMUDEZ

Roaring Brook Press
New York

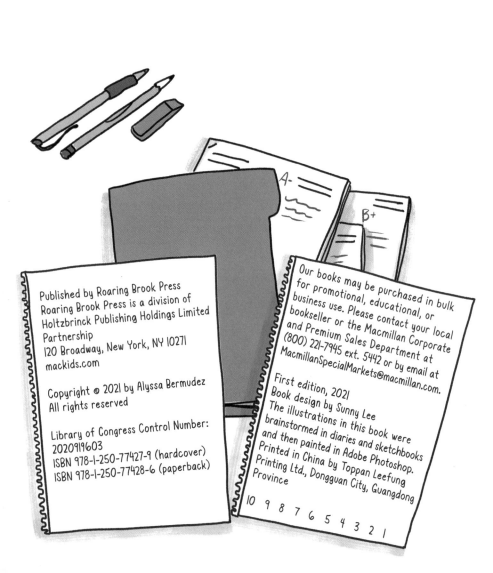

Published by Roaring Brook Press
Roaring Brook Press is a division of
Holtzbrinck Publishing Holdings Limited
Partnership
120 Broadway, New York, NY 10271
mackids.com

Copyright © 2021 by Alyssa Bermudez
All rights reserved

Library of Congress Control Number:
2020919603
ISBN 978-1-250-77427-9 (hardcover)
ISBN 978-1-250-77428-6 (paperback)

Our books may be purchased in bulk
for promotional, educational, or
business use. Please contact your local
bookseller or the Macmillan Corporate
and Premium Sales Department at
(800) 221-7945 ext. 5442 or by email at
MacmillanSpecialMarkets@macmillan.com.

First edition, 2021
Book design by Sunny Lee
The illustrations in this book were
brainstormed in diaries and sketchbooks
and then painted in Adobe Photoshop.
Printed in China by Toppan Leefung
Printing Ltd., Dongguan City, Guangdong
Province

10 9 8 7 6 5 4 3 2 1

To Linda and John

Dear Diary,

It's the first week of seventh grade.

It definitely feels different than sixth grade.

Have you seen Matt yet?! OMG, he got so cute since last year!

In the last two months everyone has seemed to grow boobs, mustaches, and popularity!

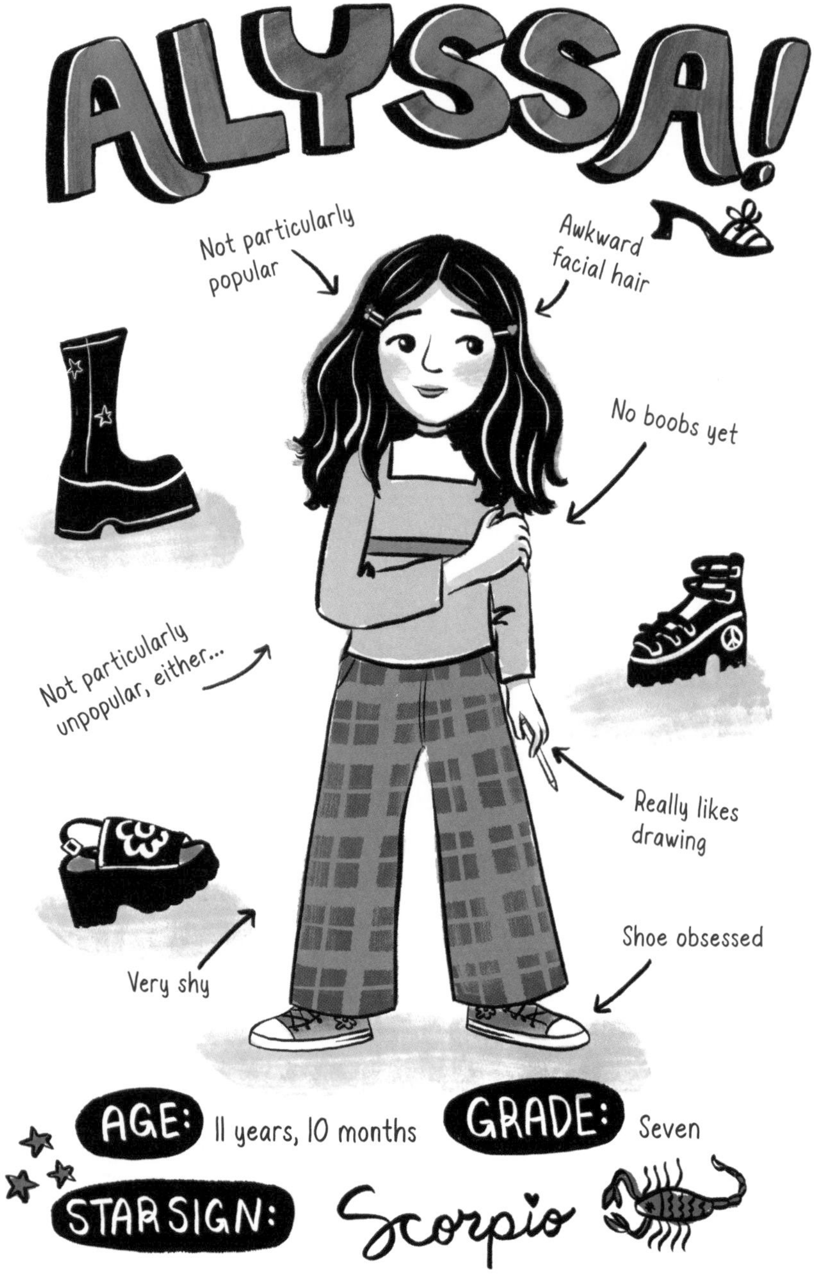
ALYSSA!
Not particularly popular
Awkward facial hair
No boobs yet
Not particularly unpopular, either...
Really likes drawing
Very shy
Shoe obsessed
AGE: 11 years, 10 months
GRADE: Seven
STAR SIGN: Scorpio

THINGS THAT ROCK MY WORLD:

CELEBRITY CRUSH VS real:

> AS LONG AS YOU LOVE ME

Brian Littrell from the Backstreet Boys.

More on him later when I have time to write again. I could probably write about him forever, but then I wouldn't get to sleep on time.

FAV. SINGERS:

MARIAH & USHER ♥

FAV. INSTRUMENT:

I am the only girl saxophone player in the school band.

WHAT I WANT TO BE SOMEDAY:

a SHOE Designer

I LOVE drawing shoes...and just drawing in general, actually!

THINGS I WANT TO DO
to change
THE WORLD :

1. Make all boys cuter and nicer
2. Stop pollution
3. Help homeless off the streets
4. Make everyone ride bikes
5. Stop wars
6. Make short people grow tall faster
7. Stop acne and periods*

*So important right now.

WHERE I LIVE:

THE WORLD:

USA ★

NYC
New York City

MANHATTAN

UPPER EAST SIDE

QUEENS

I'm in Queens with Mom.

FOREST HILLS

But also in Manhattan with Dad.

It's a long story.

The Alyssa Pie CHART

50% PUERTO RICAN

25% ITALIAN

25% BRITISH or something like that

?

MY PEOPLE:

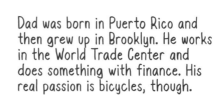

Dad was born in Puerto Rico and then grew up in Brooklyn. He works in the World Trade Center and does something with finance. His real passion is bicycles, though.

My mom grew up in Long Island but has lived in NYC for a while now. She works downtown, too, and hates it.

Siblings: It's just me! But I do have a half brother on Dad's side, Julio. He's twenty-five and plays the drums in a band. I can't wait to be his age when you can do anything you want!

BFFs:

LUCY

Lucy and I have been best friends since kindergarten. She lives four blocks away from my dad's place, is really into sports, and is always trying to do something daring and crazy, like jumping from her dresser to the bed! She somehow convinced me to do it, too, and now I have the scars to prove it.

OUCH!

CARMEN

Carmen is a newer BFF since she transferred to our school three years ago. She is a really good student and is super silly. Her family is from Puerto Rico, too, which is how we first bonded. She lives all the way in the Bronx, though, so we don't get to hang out as often as Lucy and I can.

Popular Kids:

- Can hang out whenever they want and go online whenever they want
- The nerdy boys are all terrified of them

MICHELLE

LAUREN

- Has an older brother so is immediately cool with the eighth graders, too

JANICE

- Not shy
- Teacher's pet
- Cool style

- Athletic
- Rich
- Not boring

EDDIE

- Not shy

JOEY

MARTY

- Class clown
- Always making fun of everyone, including ME for not speaking Spanish and being a "Fake Puerto Rican"

- Funny
- Has freedom

We've all been together at St. Ignatius for about seven years! It's a Catholic school on 84th Street.

PROS

1. All of my friends are here, and everyone knows everyone.
2. I've had the same art teacher for seven years now and he's the best!
3. Alejandro.
4. There is a good pizza place on the corner, Mimi's, where everyone who is popular hangs out after school.

CONS

1. The detention-worthy rules—no makeup, no nail polish, no hair dye, not too many hair clips, no platform shoes allowed.
2. We have to go to church all the time and study for our confirmation this year.
3. Nuns live on the top floor and it's really scary up there.
4. Our teachers are extra hard on us now that our grades are important for high school applications.
5. No one else loves drawing as much as I do so I can't really talk about it with anyone.
6. There's no outside recreation area like the schools I see on TV shows, so we usually hang out on the street in the front.

"BOTTLE CAP HOCKEY"

Popularity was never such a big deal until now. It used to be so much easier. All Lucy ever needed was a really cool birthday party at the ice rink to make everyone like her. Now it takes a lot more effort, and I just don't think I'm cut out for it.

It seems that suddenly every grade you get and everything you do matters. Our teachers and parents want us to get the best grades to get into a good high school. Now our friends are obsessed with who has a crush on who, and who is the coolest. There is all of this pressure to be popular and smart or face a dim future being a weirdo with no job.

On top of this, it's so hard to make a good impression when you're not allowed to do anything EVER. I wish that I had more freedom to hang out or go online. Michelle, Lauren, and Marty are always hanging out after school and on weekends. I have to call Mom at her office by 4 PM every day or else she'll go crazy. After that I try to sneak online for a little while.

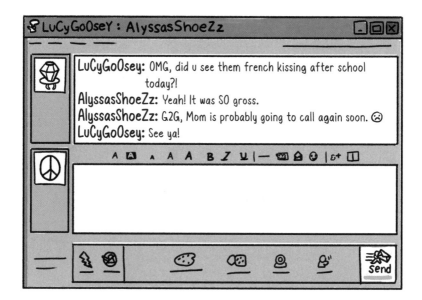

your NOT-SO-COOL writer,

alyssa

It's hard to be popular when I can't hang out with my friends, and it's even harder to do that when I live in two places! I've been going back and forth like this since second grade. At first my mom and I stayed in the Upper East Side apartment while Dad stayed in a studio downtown. I didn't realize it was a big deal until later because everything else sort of continued as usual. Until one day, on the way to school...

It's the only time I've seen Dad cry that I can remember.

After the separation, they made it official. Mom asked me if I would mind moving to Queens with her. I thought it would be like the country or something. The high schools there have outdoor fields and big campuses! I don't mind going back and forth to our different apartments because both feel like home. It mostly becomes a problem when I forget to bring something important to one home or the other.

WEEKEND BAG

Dear Diary,

And then there is *Alejandro*

Neither popular nor unpopular, like me.

I have to introduce you to Alejandro before I tell you the BEST THING EVER. I haven't told you much about him yet because I wanted to try and find my favorite pen and some time before bed to write all of the details.

Regular pen
to write about
regular things

Favorite pen
(Can't be found
ANYWHERE)

But he is just too amazing to wait any longer!

The first second I saw him, on September 18, 1998, I knew I liked him.

OMG

We have a new student from Colombia! Please welcome him and be kind to him as he adjusts to our school and language.

And there he was...

- Beautiful eyelashes

- Green eyes

- Dark hair

He looked a bit sad that day, but mostly cute.

His father is the ambassador of Colombia and that's why they moved here.

E 84st

ONE WAY

Every morning and every afternoon he is escorted in a black town car and it is very mysterious.

He has no freedom, like me!

He isn't very popular and never hangs out after school.
In fact, he's even shyer than I am, if that's physically possible.
I want to go near him, but my legs don't move anywhere. When
he comes toward me my legs just start to move away.

It's like one heart against a million other parts of my body.

I have no control!

Today in school a

SPECTACULAR

miracle occurred...despite how it started:

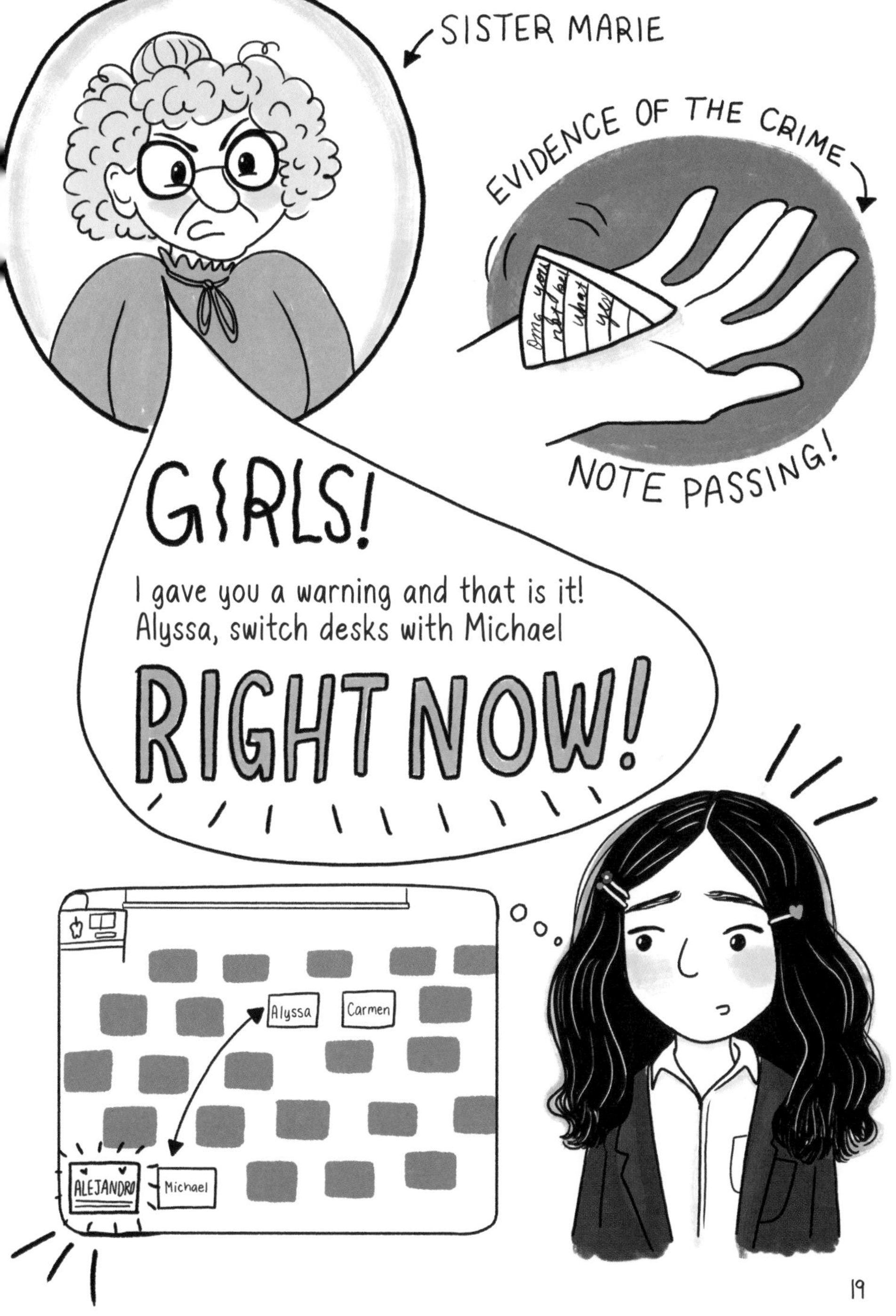
SISTER MARIE
EVIDENCE OF THE CRIME
NOTE PASSING!
GIRLS!
I gave you a warning and that is it!
Alyssa, switch desks with Michael
RIGHT NOW!
Alyssa
Carmen
ALEJANDRO
Michael

SCREECH

SCRATCH

Alejandro

Approx. 12 inches distance

alyssa

ALEJANDRO AND I ARE NOW DESKMATES!

That's right, we sit next to each other every single day for four out of eight classes now! That's at least 180 minutes of being in extremely close proximity to him.

Breathing the same air!

I'm NEVER in trouble at school so I would consider this to be divine intervention.

Our feet on the same floor tile.

It turns out the whole desk miracle was actually the beginning of a disaster. The only person in the entire world who knew I had a crush on Alejandro was my mom.

After the desk swap, I told Carmen and Janice the big secret, too.

Later that day, Janice came over to my desk at break time and Alejandro decided to stay and read instead of move toward his friends.

You know who likes you, Alejandro?

Alyssa does!

She loves your green eyes and she was happy when she got to sit next to you, and she has liked you since the first day you came here!

Oh...

I sat there stunned as a statue.

Yeah, she loves you.

After Janice left, Alejandro and I sat side by side in awkward silence.

I had to say something. But what? Nothing could make it less awkward. I wanted to crawl up in a ball and disappear.

I had to clear the air! I mustered up all of my courage and told him the truth.

Look, Alejandro...

I don't love you, I just like you a lot.

Since Janice spoke the words out loud, literally EVERYONE at school found out. Now even all of our teachers know, too. Everyone keeps on bugging me about it.

I was grateful for prayer time...so everyone could stop making fun of us for a moment!

At least I don't think he dislikes me. The clues are:

1. He doesn't want to move desks next to someone else.
2. I catch him glancing at me sometimes.
3. At break he doesn't move next to his friends. He stays right there. Carmen and Janice come over by me during breaks and tell him to go somewhere else if he wants to, but he always says, "No, that's okay."

You never know, maybe he does like me.

The Alejandro Lover,
Alyssa

November 1st, 2000

It's almost my birthday and that means I get to go shopping for a special outfit! Grandma always sends me a birthday outfit from Puerto Rico, which I am obligated to take photos in, but this year I get to choose what I like, too!

November 11th, 2000

It's my birthday!

ice cream cake

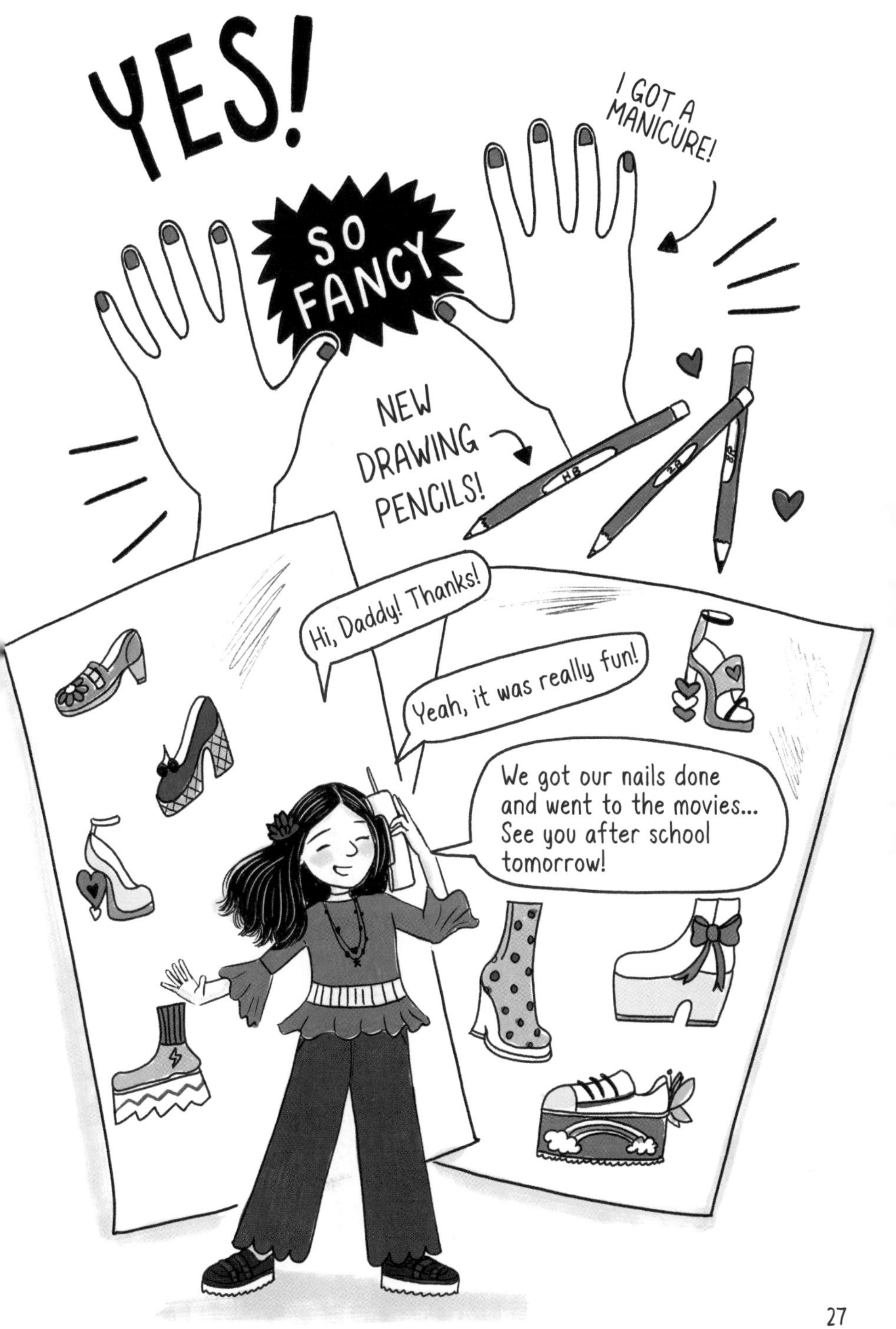

YES!
I GOT A MANICURE!
SO FANCY
NEW DRAWING PENCILS!
HB
2B
6B
Hi, Daddy! Thanks!
Yeah, it was really fun!
We got our nails done and went to the movies... See you after school tomorrow!

Being twelve is one step closer to freedom! Mom and Dad are finally letting me take the subway by myself—at least part of the way. First, Mom and I take the train together from our stop in Forest Hills, Queens, to 59th Street in Manhattan.

From there I go by myself to the connecting 4/5/6 train to get to 86th Street.

At first I felt a bit nervous, but I've been riding the subway my whole life so I definitely knew what to expect.

Common Sights on the SUBWAY:

THE NAIL CLIPPER

THE MUSIC BLASTER

THE PREACHER

THE WEIRD PET

THE ACTRESS

THE SANTAS

THE ACROBATS

THE INNOVATORS

THE HEAD BOBBERS
(This was me once.)

leftover coffee cups

When you see a Safe Haven sign on a store window, it means you can find a helpful grown-up in there if you are in trouble.

When I start high school I'll probably take the subway to and from everywhere. A lot of city kids go to high school across boroughs and commute for an hour each way! Who knows what high school I'll end up in...

THE FIVE BOROUGHS

Your city slicker,
Alyssa

Dear Diary,

So this week started off like a nightmare.

I was just SO MAD at my face!

My eyebrows had been torturing me for months now. I'm sure everyone else has noticed, too, considering they look like kissing caterpillars trying to take over my head.

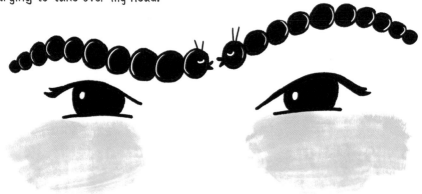

Mom said when I'm older, I can get them waxed...
But last night after I stared at them in the mirror
one last time, I knew I couldn't wait.

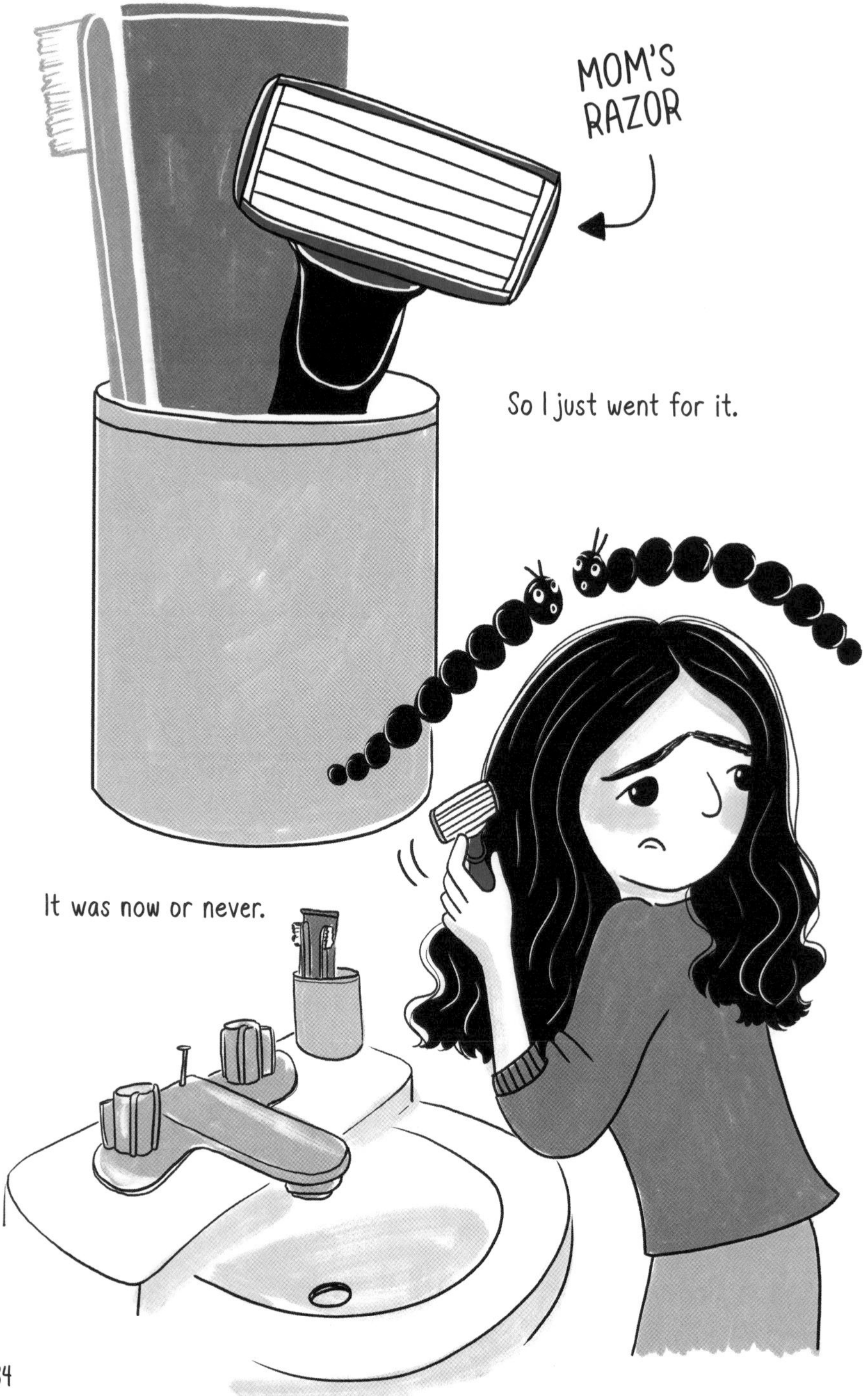
MOM'S RAZOR
So I just went for it.
It was now or never.

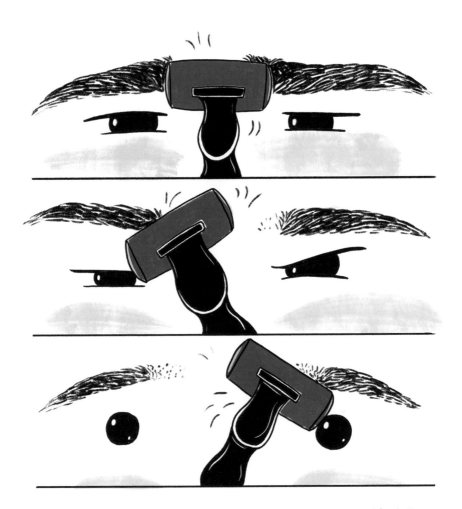

Then I realized they were uneven, so I shaved a little more off of the other side, then back again to the first side. I went back and forth like this until I discovered I shaved off WAY more eyebrow than needed.

I went straight to bed and pretended it was a dream.

The next morning, my plan was to avoid everyone.

Starting with MOM.

Then on the way to school...

At school there is a strict NO HATS policy, so I had to bury my head in books...

I managed to find excuses at break time and lunch.

CRUNCH

Aren't you coming??

I just need to catch up on that thing, you know, the one that I got a bad grade on, and I don't want a progress report so I am doing extra credit—

But of course nothing gets by Lauren and Michelle, so soon enough the secret was out.

Um, Alyssa, what's up with your face today? Did you, like, fall asleep on a weed whacker or something?

YO! THAT'S COLD!

HAHA HAHA!

It's not that bad, I swear! It will grow back soon probably.

After spinning in a **BLACK HOLE** of regret at school, I then had to face my mother back at home **AGAIN.**

And NOTHING gets past her twice.

Mom's All-Seeing Eye

WHAT DID YOU DO?!

To top it all off, I then had to hear all about the dangers of putting a razor to one's face and how horrified she was. Now she thinks I'm going to do other crazy stuff and doesn't trust me.

Living with this face is punishment enough!

Your regretful writer,
Alyssa

November 24th, 2000

Thank GOD it's Thanksgiving break and I can finally have some peace from the school gossipers. This year I spent it with my dad. He's not much of a cook so he ordered in for the two of us. My half brother, Julio, spent Thanksgiving with his mom. My mom spent it with one of her friends. I guess for other people it seems a bit complicated, but we have it pretty organized.

This year I was thankful for remembering to bring enough supplies for the weekend so I didn't have to have another horrendous conversation with Dad about "girls needing certain things as they are going through puberty."

After Thanksgiving dinner was over I headed to Lucy's apartment. When I walked through the door it immediately smelled amazing, and also felt strange to me, like I was watching a family on a TV show. There were at least a dozen people there, and most of them were still sitting around the table. Everything was decorated and every person was loud.

I almost managed to get on their Thanksgiving race tournament board, but Lucy beat me, like usual.

Sometimes I wish I had a normal family like theirs.

Your thankful writer,
Alyssa

December 4th, 2000

Today we had our last Girl Scout troop meeting of the year after school.

Our troop leader organized packages for us to give to women in need, and we even found a way to sneak in some beauty tips! Carmen and I created this booklet to show the ladies how they can apply makeup for job interviews. Carmen knows all about makeup from her dance school, so I trust that it makes sense. I LOVE drawing faces. Just because I can't wear makeup yet doesn't mean I can't draw it!

What are they even doing over there?

It looks SO stupid.

I felt SO embarrassed. I really like Girl Scouts even if other people think it's dorky. I've been in this troop since second grade and we've done some really cool things!

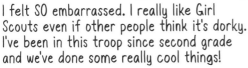

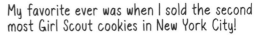
My favorite ever was when I sold the second most Girl Scout cookies in New York City!

Dad had a pretty good strategy since he works in the World Trade Center, which is such a big building.

We started at the top floor and visited each cubicle.

Hi, my name is Alyssa Bermudez from troop 3306. Would you be interested in buying some Girl Scout cookies?

46

ORDERS

Four boxes of Samoas, please!

75

One for me, too!

46

Three boxes of Thin Mints... OH! And one Tagalong, please!

32

27

We went to nearly every floor together until I had more than 1,000 orders.

When it came time to deliver the cookies we soon realized there was a much bigger problem.

All of these cookies had to be brought downtown to Dad's office.

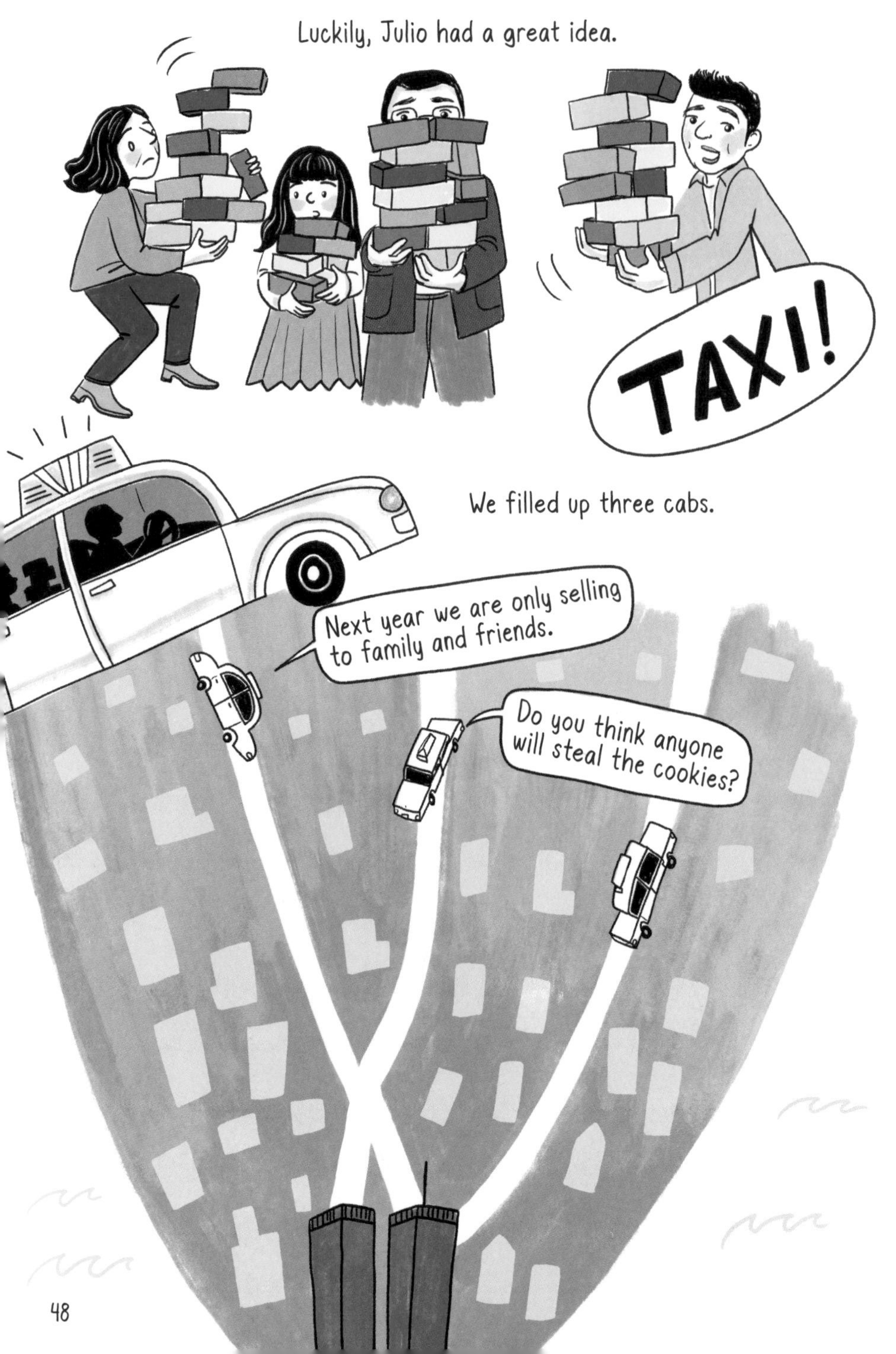
Luckily, Julio had a great idea.
TAXI!
We filled up three cabs.
Next year we are only selling to family and friends.
Do you think anyone will steal the cookies?

December 10th, 2000

There are only fifteen days until Christmas! We got a Social Studies test back today, which I didn't really study for, and I did NOT do well. I just hid it in a folder to make sure Mom never sees. As long as I do well next time my average will probably still be fine.

Mom and I decorated the tree at her apartment tonight. It came out pretty nice! The good thing about living in Queens is that we have a bit more space than at Dad's apartment in Manhattan. He doesn't even get a tree there anymore.

Everything was going well until dinner came...

AS IF! Having my twenty-five-year-old brother watching me and my friends BOWLING seems like a social disaster.

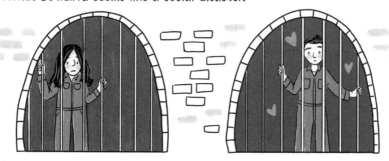

Alejandro's probably not going, either, so I guess it's okay. Another day in the life in big city prison.

ZERO FREEDOM CHIC:

ESCAPE SHOES

HOME

BØYS

★ · ♥ · ★ · ♥ · ★ · ♥ · ★ · ♥ · ★ ·

I heard from Carmen that Alejandro's friend James told her that Alejandro told HIM that I was really good at drawing. That totally means he notices me! I am definitely going to draw more in school now.

BROUGHT TO YOU BY ALYSSA AND LOVE!

December 20th, 2000

I survived today! But barely. Everyone was so happy and cheerful at school, even Sister Marie for once! Lucy, Carmen, and I exchanged gifts.

All I could think about was Alejandro's Christmas card weighing down my whole brain. It took me ALL DAY to figure it out.

How was I going to give it to him?!

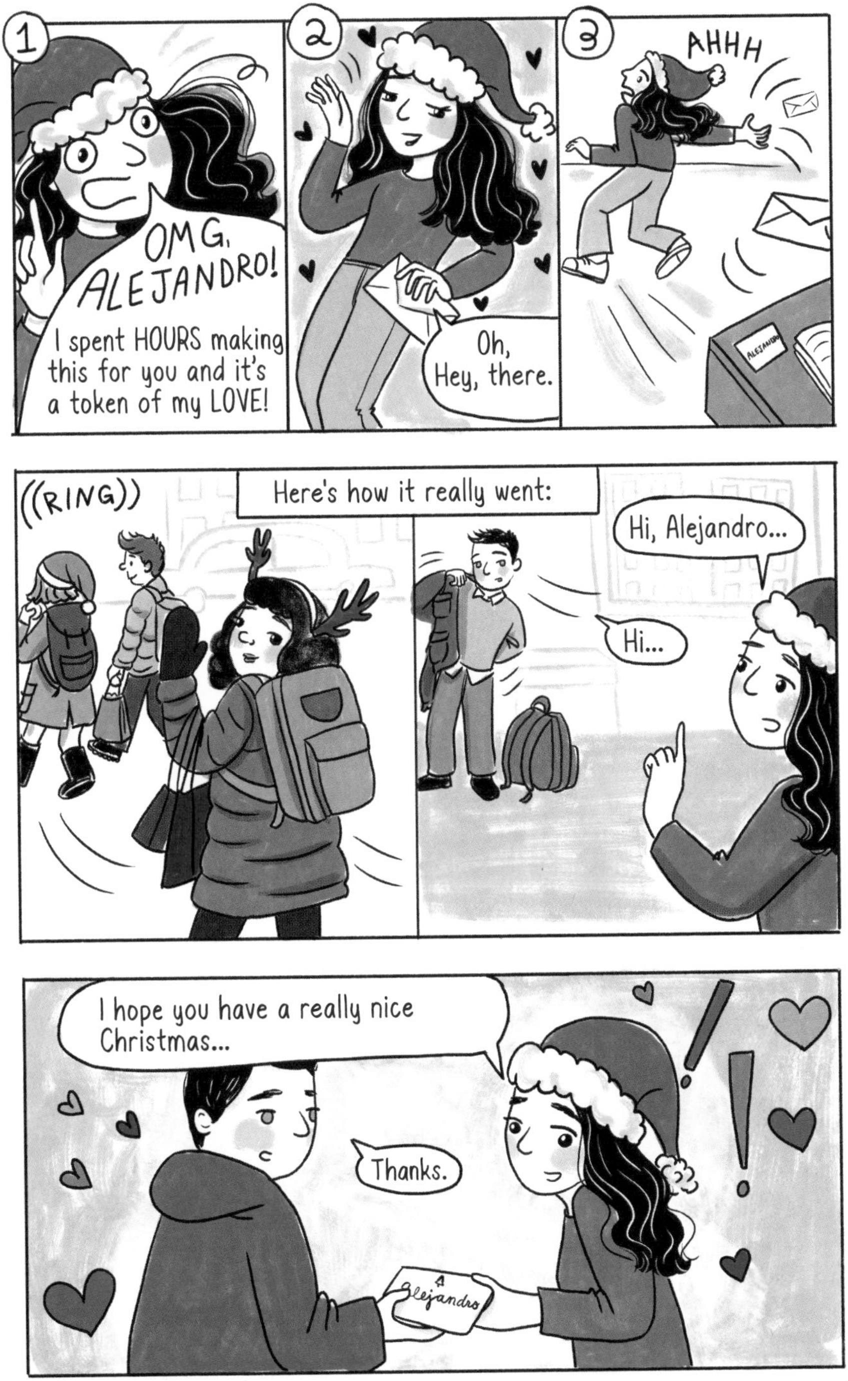
1
OMG, ALEJANDRO!
I spent HOURS making this for you and it's a token of my LOVE!
2
Oh, Hey, there.
3
AHHH
ALEJANDRO
((RING))
Here's how it really went:
Hi, Alejandro...
Hi...
I hope you have a really nice Christmas...
Thanks.
Alejandro

I brought my big bag to school so I could go directly to Dad's for Christmas week. Walking home with all of my stuff AND Christmas presents was pretty embarrassing.

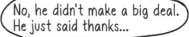

Hi, Mom. Yes, I'm at Dad's now...

No, he didn't make a big deal. He just said thanks...

Yeah, I'll only practice the saxophone during work hours...

I KNOW it's loud for the neighbors... Okay, yeah. Love you, too.

Dad and I have our usual plans for Christmas. We always go to FAO Schwarz and Rockefeller Center.

Dad always brings his special camera and takes photos of me with the gigantic toys and tree. I'm definitely too old for it now, but I'm excited anyway.

It's dorky and cute how happy it makes Dad. I just hope I don't run into ANYONE from school.

Julio will probably come to have dinner with us, but the rest of the day is just for the two of us.

YAY

Today I went back to Mom's for Christmas Eve and we stayed up until midnight to open presents. I got the shoes I was DYING over. Mom originally said "NO WAY" about their chunky platform heel, thinking I would break an ankle or something.

I put them in a special place in the closet near my other favorite shoes. One pair is from the '80s! Mom almost got rid of them when she was cleaning stuff out. How can anyone get rid of shoes?!

WOW

MOM'S '80s SHOES

Here's what I got

Here's what Mom got

December 26th, 2000

Christmas with Dad was great!

hola

(Dad buys frozen pasteles from Carmen's grandma)

Pasteles are a Puerto Rican Christmas dish

Dad thinks I should start going to the Met art classes for middle school kids on Saturdays. Apparently they are free, so both of my parents agree it's a good place to start. I'm not sure how I feel about it, though, since I won't know anyone there. What if everyone is weird? Or what if they all think I am the weird one?

Maybe I will try to work on my Spanish during the New Year, too, since I was too embarrassed to speak in Spanish to Grandma yesterday on the phone. I feel so disconnected from this side of myself, and I wonder if speaking more Spanish will help. I just feel mortified if I make a mistake and say something wrong. You know who could be my tutor? Alejandro. I'm going to cut this entry short to see if he's online now. This could be a good topic to bring up to him.

an ALEJANDRO UPDATE

NO LUCK ON THE ONLINE FRONT.

SCENE I

Alejandro FAN FICTION

Time: 9:30 PM
Setting: Movies

Alyssa is watching a movie with her new amazing boyfriend, Alejandro.

His hand slowly goes over toward hers.

She sees what he is about to do.

She gets a funny feeling...

After much anticipation, they finally start holding hands.

Alyssa eats popcorn and she puts a kernel in his mouth. She starts feeding him. He puts one in her mouth, too.

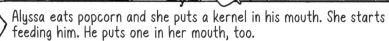

Pure bliss.

This movie is boring.

Yeah, it is.

What will she think if I put my arm around her?

Alejandro very slowly does just that.

Your eyes are WONDERFUL.

YOU are wonderful.

the end

December 31st, 2000

It's the very last day of the year and since I am spending New Year's with Dad I got to invite Lucy and Carmen over for the day. We had some very important plans on our itinerary, including our yearly outing: Eating Ice Cream on the Coldest Day of the Year.

We still have seven days before school starts again and that means we can wear nail polish until then! Dad got nail polish remover for his apartment after hearing about my detention incident.

NEW YEAR RESOLUTIONS:

BE LESS SHY

BLAH! BLAH!

DRAW MORE

Shoes

BOOTS

FACES

GET BETTER GRADES

CARPE DIEM!
LATIN
SCIENCE
SOCIAL STUDIES
MATH

2001

January 3rd, 2001

First entry of 2001! I'm sort of off to a really strange start.

Yesterday I went to Dad's office with him since I am still on Christmas vacation. There is a program there for kids during vacation time, so Dad dropped me off there.

It was slightly mortifying because I felt like I was WAY too old for this supervised day.

I imagined what all of the other kids from school were doing, but I didn't want to make Dad feel bad about it since he paid for me to be there.

After about a half hour, there were a surprising number of kids around my age.

We got on the bus to go to the planetarium and that's when things started to get strange...

Oh, you guys play soccer? Me, too!

Cool! What position do you play?

WHAT ON EARTH AM I DOING?!

SPORTS ?? POSITIONS ?? SHOES?

...no idea

Umm...it depends.

Nice! I'm going to soccer camp this year...I usually play left forward.

It's like an alien just took over my body and started talking about things that have never happened to me before.

I'm not sure why I just kept going. I hate sports and I have never broken a bone! Perhaps I realized that I would never see these people again, and I just wanted to make my life sound more exciting for once. I guess in some way it was fulfilling my "be less shy" New Year's resolution, but it's not really how I expected it to go. I had the urge to try and fit in, but I felt so icky afterward. I definitely won't be trying that again.

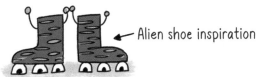
Alien shoe inspiration

Your shameful writer,
Alyssa

an ALEJANDRO UPDATE

He was online at the same time so I said, "Hola!" He said, "Hola lol!" Is that flirting?!

Dear Diary,

OMG, I am going to be in BIG trouble. Now that school is back, we got our test grades back from before Christmas. I did NOT do well and it's not the first time this year.

What's worse is that I left my big bonus points assignment at Dad's so I couldn't hand it in on time. Mom is always telling me to get organized and write things down so I don't forget, but she doesn't know how difficult and annoying it is to keep track of everything in TWO homes.

It looks like I am going to have to study ALL night, EVERY DAY to get a better average from now on.

It might already be too late! Goodbye, already nonexistent social life.

Once my parents find out, it will actually be the end of everything. Worst of all, I really let myself down. Now that every grade will be looked at by high schools, I might not even get accepted to any of my top picks!

I'll have to tell Mom tomorrow because she has to sign my tests by Friday.

January 9th, 2001

Everyone at school is talking about the winter dance coming up. I still can't focus on that while the whole academic world is crumbling around me. I am about to tell Mom about my grades. If I die and this is my last diary entry, whoever finds this has my permission to drop it in the deepest ocean for no one to ever see again.

January 10th, 2001

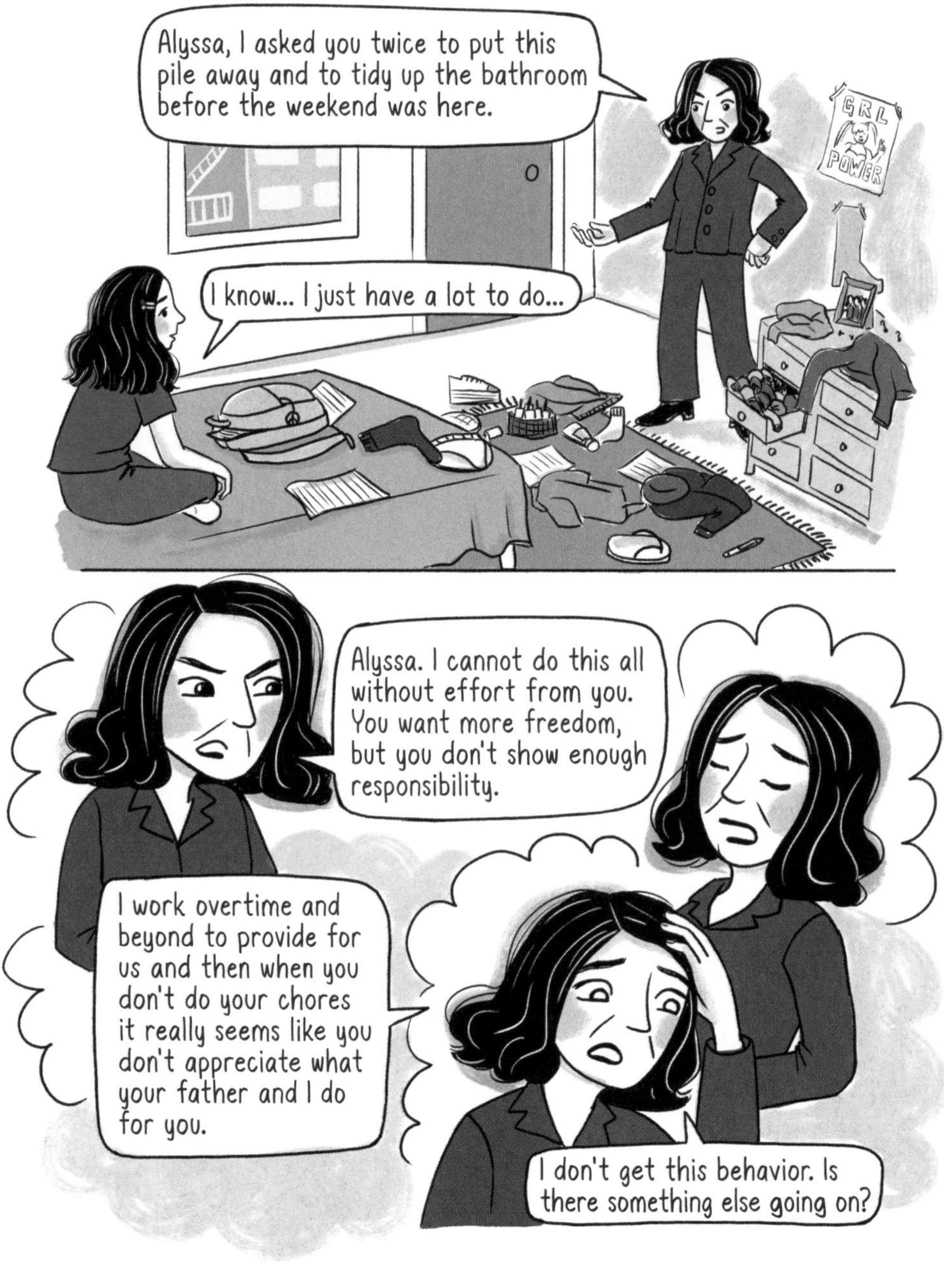

Alyssa, I asked you twice to put this pile away and to tidy up the bathroom before the weekend was here.
I know... I just have a lot to do...
GRL POWER
Alyssa. I cannot do this all without effort from you. You want more freedom, but you don't show enough responsibility.
I work overtime and beyond to provide for us and then when you don't do your chores it really seems like you don't appreciate what your father and I do for you.
I don't get this behavior. Is there something else going on?

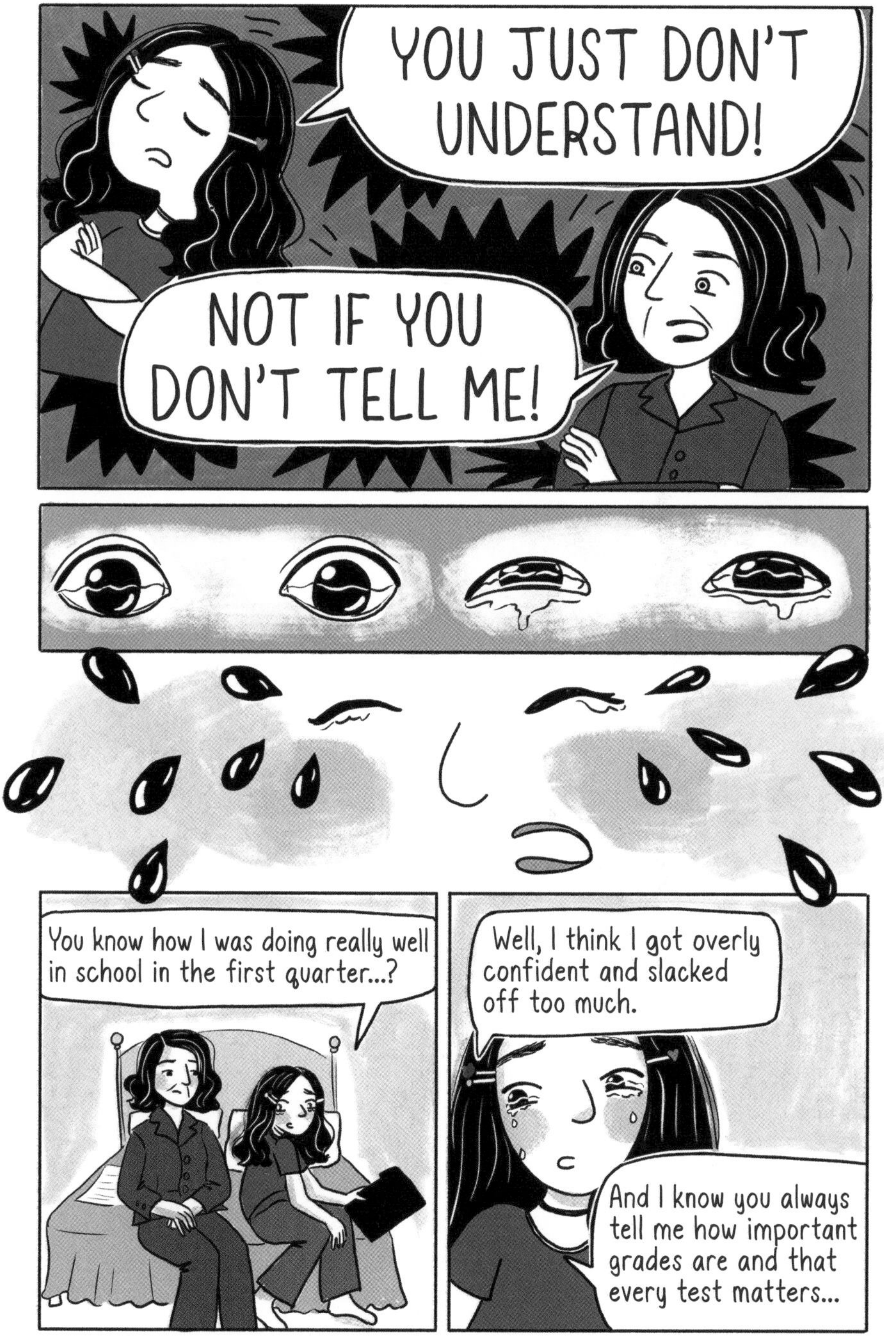
YOU JUST DON'T UNDERSTAND!
NOT IF YOU DON'T TELL ME!
You know how I was doing really well in school in the first quarter...?
Well, I think I got overly confident and slacked off too much.
And I know you always tell me how important grades are and that every test matters...

I could tell she was disappointed, but we came up with a plan for each subject. She told me I have to put my grades before my friends and everything else, otherwise my online time will be reduced to NIL.

Meanwhile, I can't focus because the thought of Alejandro is so distracting!

His arm grazed mine when he raised his hand in class. Neither of us EVER raise our hands in class, so I considered that a pretty good sign of what's to come.

January 17th, 2001

The winter dance is three DAYS away. I want to go, but I promised Mom and Dad I would do well on my next two tests. I got an essay back today and I'm off to a good start!

I know I should feel happy, and usually I do. Things are turning around, but sometimes I just feel really sad, ugly, and lonely. It's almost too terrible to even write in words, but I do usually feel better after writing in my diary and doing some drawing. Sometimes I feel really mature, and other times I feel so down in the dumps where it's just too hard to tell anyone. I want to show my parents that I can be responsible, and I want to show my friends at school that there is more to me.

January 19th 2001

With everything going on I almost forgot about the dance coming up!
I haven't even decided on an outfit! It's time to focus on something
happy—fashion! I am also crossing my fingers that I won't wake up with
a million zits. Twenty-four-hour dance countdown begins now!

These make the perfect CLICK-CLACK sound when I dance.

You can't go wrong with a CHIC black turtleneck.

January 20th, 2001

What a night! Where to begin...

Everyone was there. Michelle, Lauren, and Janice were dancing in the middle of everyone as if they were movie stars onstage.

Once there were more people, it was easier to sort of blend in.

I casually scanned the room to see where Alejandro was.

He looked so cute in his dark blue shirt.

We were all just dancing and being silly, until a slow song came on.

YANK

SHOVE

PULL

I was terrified.

I used all of my bravery in one split second.

He followed by putting his hands on my waist and finally everyone left us alone.

I don't even remember what song it was because I was temporarily unable to process or hear anything.

Once the song was over, I let go and smiled at him before running away very quickly.

I was on cloud nine for the whole night.

Dear Diary,

Maybe one day I'll have a real first kiss. The kind that no one has to push and shove you into.

Today I unfortunately kissed someone outside at recess. It's not what you think, though... It's not Alejandro. It's actually much, much worse.

But that didn't matter to them. Suddenly everyone was surrounding us!

I had to make it stop! So I just did it!

As the day continued, it just got worse and worse. Matt thought I ran away because I was upset with him, but he didn't understand that I felt so pressured and there were so many people! I just wanted it to stop!

Why can't I just say NO to things like this? I didn't want to kiss him in the first place!

HA HA

Sucking face with Matt!

I wish I had a better kissing story to compare it to, but my very first kiss was even WORSE and also a dare.

FLASHBACK
—SIX MONTHS AGO—

After Marty's birthday party in May, we were all getting dropped off at home: truth or dare AGAIN.

Z Z Z

Eddie!

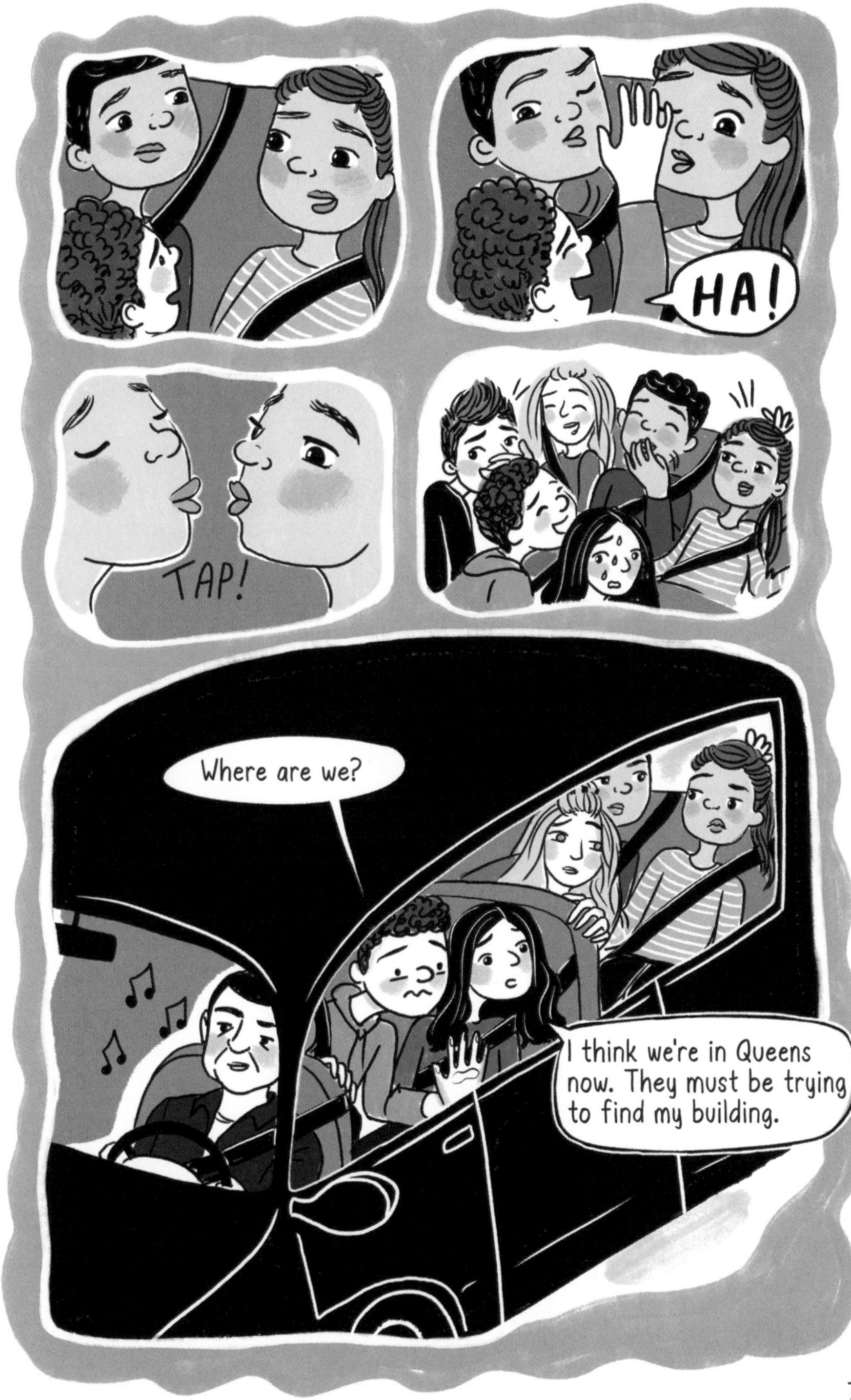
HA!
TAP!
Where are we?
I think we're in Queens now. They must be trying to find my building.

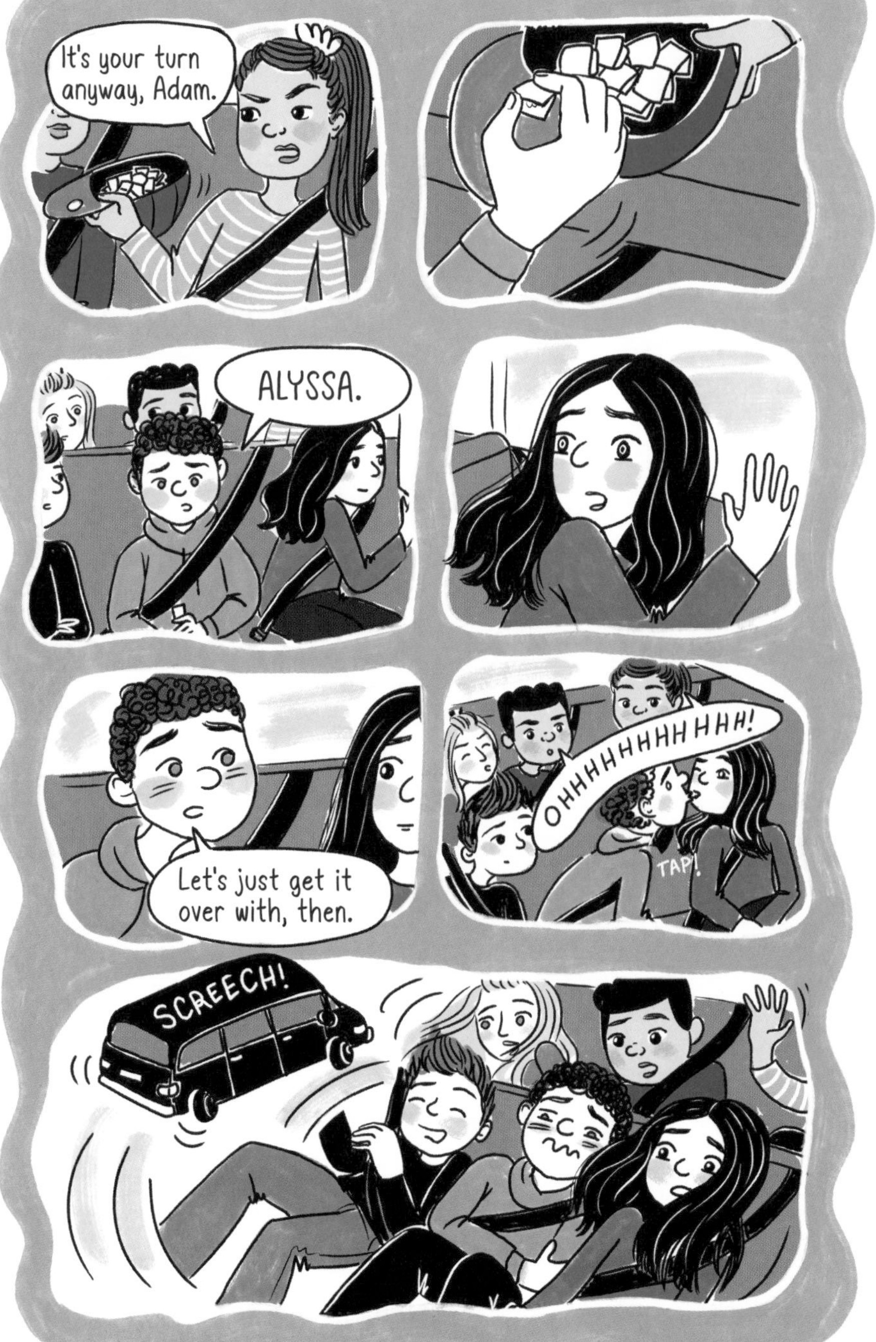
It's your turn anyway, Adam.
ALYSSA.
Let's just get it over with, then.
OHHHHHHHHHHH!
TAP!
SCREECH!

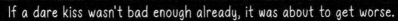

It was NOT the first kiss I had imagined. I had to hear the barf story for weeks. Hopefully one day, I get a real first kiss.

The bad-luck kisser,
alyssa

February 1st, 2001

Luckily everyone has forgotten about the kissing by now and is worried about Valentine's Day instead.

I wish Alejandro would ask me to be his valentine. Everyone wants Alejandro to ask me, but I don't think they should force him. Because if he doesn't like me by now, he probably never will!

Carmen gave me her two photos of me and Alejandro dancing. One is already taped onto the wall and the other one I'll put in this diary.

February 6th, 2001

Yesterday I did something very stupid. I knew it was stupid at the time and I still did it anyway. It's like the drive to be popular makes me see things through stupid lenses.

We were in band practice like we are every Monday and the older boys were goofing off.

Before our teacher entered the room, the boys said they were ditching practice and going out instead.

Are you girls coming or what?

We had to decide quickly before our band teacher arrived. Carmen got up first and I followed her. I had never cut class or an extracurricular before.

We sat in the pizza place for an hour while everyone chatted. I could tell Carmen had a crush on one of the older guys.

Time was ticking and we had to sneak back into school for pickups.

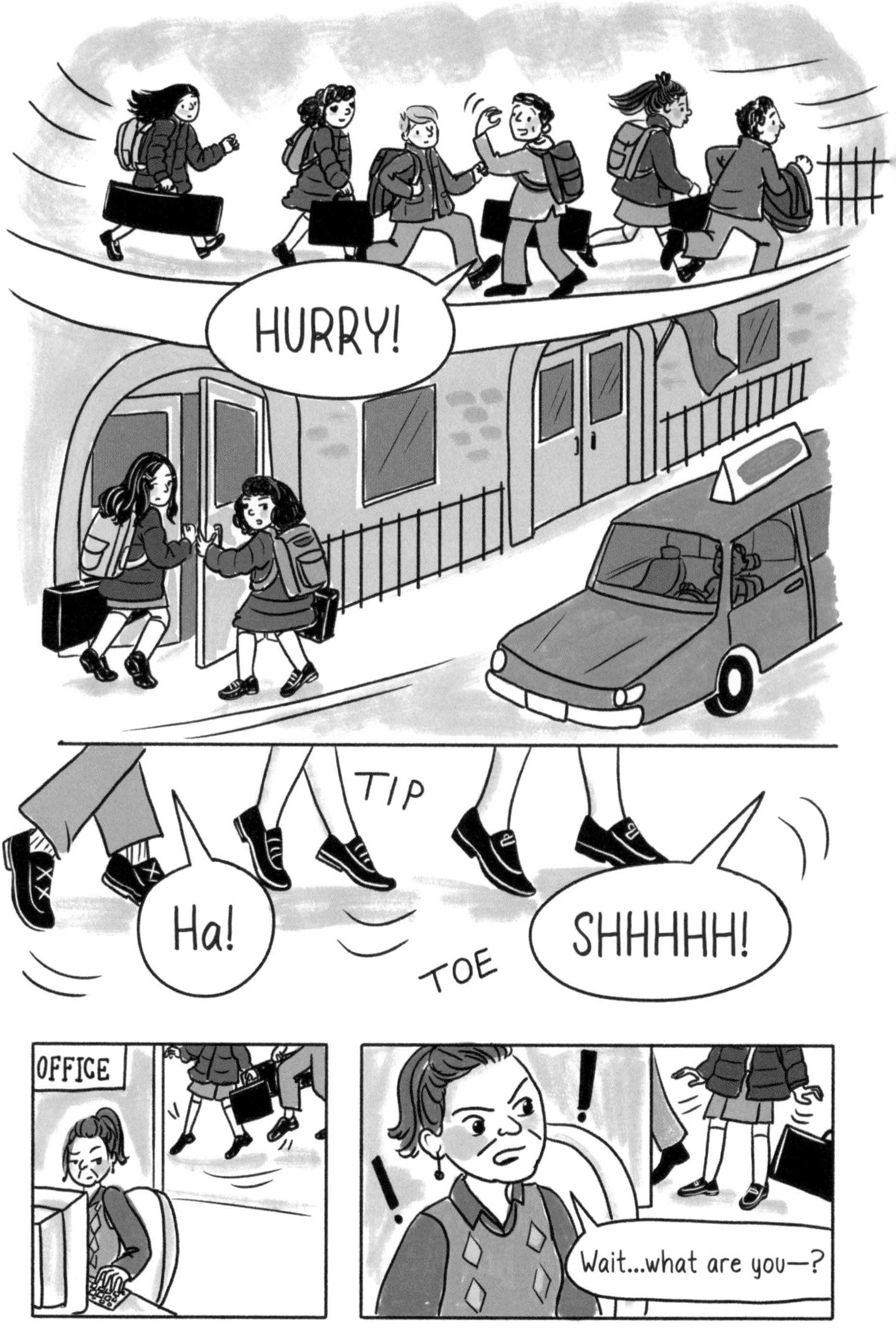
HURRY!
TIP
Ha!
TOE
SHHHHH!
OFFICE
!
!
Wait...what are you—?

My parents say I will be grounded for a while and I have to get them to trust me again. I am only tempted to do things because everyone else seems to be allowed to do anything they want. I don't even like the older guys in band, but everyone just turns stupid around them! I didn't want to be left out.

I feel all of this pressure to be good, but when I do one thing wrong, everyone loses trust in me. Now I have a reputation of being bad!

I feel so terrible inside. I am so sad sometimes that I just want to curl up in bed. Dad says maybe I'm not mature enough to do the summer trip he is planning and that we should wait until I'm older. I hate disappointing him.

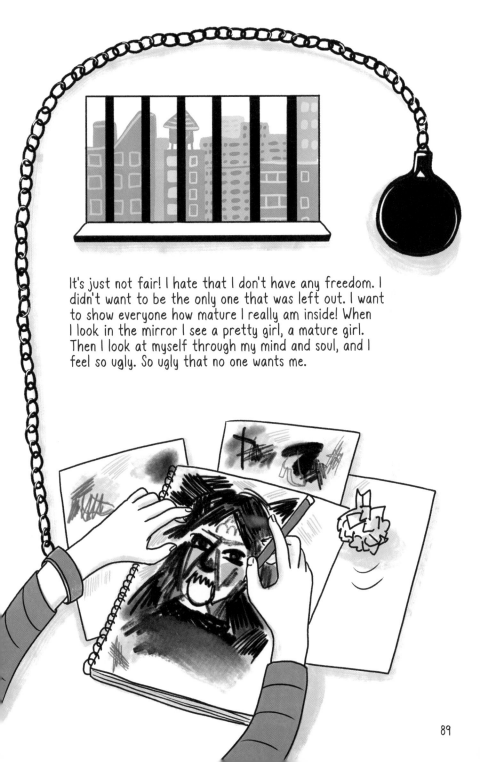

It's just not fair! I hate that I don't have any freedom. I didn't want to be the only one that was left out. I want to show everyone how mature I really am inside! When I look in the mirror I see a pretty girl, a mature girl. Then I look at myself through my mind and soul, and I feel so ugly. So ugly that no one wants me.

89

February 10th, 2001

After spending time drawing, I actually feel a bit better and have accepted my fate of not being allowed to do anything ever.

SNOW BOOTS

BICYCLE SHOES

RAIN BOOTS

CAN GO ON ANY SHOE

PLATFORM GALOSHES

A+A

With Valentine's Day coming up, I can also easily distract myself with romantic thoughts of Alejandro and me on an imaginary date!

your loved-up writer,
alyssa

February 14th, 2001

 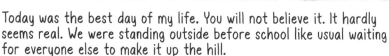

an Alejandro UPDATE OH, MY GOSH!

Today was the best day of my life. You will not believe it. It hardly seems real. We were standing outside before school like usual waiting for everyone else to make it up the hill.

Whoa...is that Alejandro?

That's when we all saw that he was carrying a rose. I started curling up into a ball and dying on the inside imagining the torture of having to watch him give it to someone.

Happy Valentine's Day...

The rose was for me.

It was the most beautiful flower I've ever seen. Just thinking about that moment again makes me giggle and want to scream.

Soon the whole school found out about it.

Even Sister Marie knows!

It was SO embarrassing. Alejandro is probably going to go back into his hole and never do anything romantic ever again. As soon as I got to Dad's apartment after school, I called Mom and told her. She was so excited, too, and then told everyone around her at work, so now the whole universe knows.

HAVE YOU HEARD?

OMG!

WHAT?

I can't believe he was brave enough to do that! I mean, he's so shy! I have a feeling one of his friends convinced him. Whoever it was, I am forever grateful.

your loved-up Valentine, Alyssa

February 28th, 2001

Today at school we went to church for Ash Wednesday.

After the rose, I thought everything might change for me. But Alejandro hasn't really spoken to me more since Valentine's Day other than "Hi" and "Bye."

I'm worried that someone dared him to give me the rose and he's just too nice to admit it. He probably felt bad for me and now things are worse than ever!

If only things could work out like they do in the movies.

I wish Janice didn't tell all of our teachers that I like Alejandro! Everyone teases him about it and he probably thinks that I told them myself! That must be why he doesn't like me and gave me a pity rose!

March 3rd, 2001

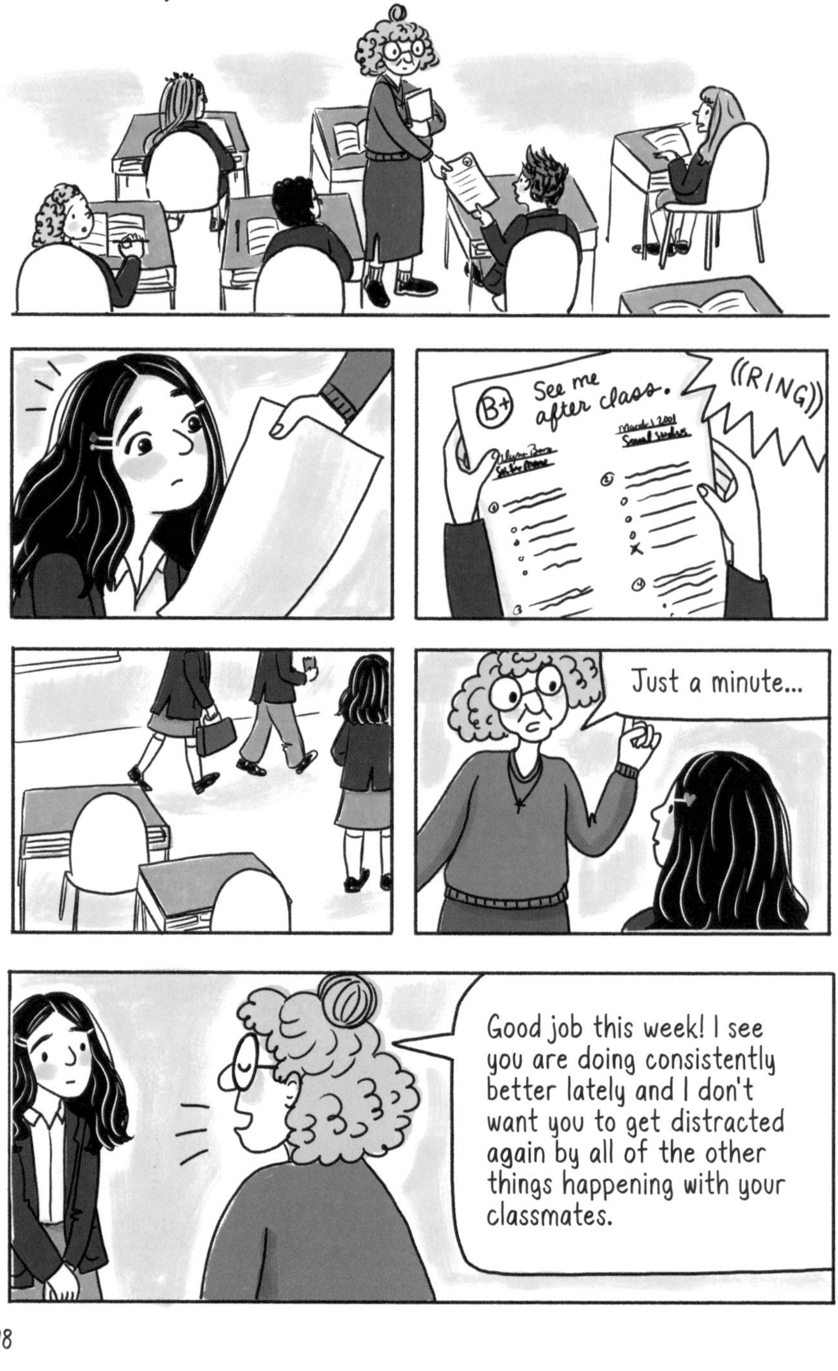
B+
See me after class.
((RING))
Just a minute...
Good job this week! I see you are doing consistently better lately and I don't want you to get distracted again by all of the other things happening with your classmates.

Another All-Seeing Eye

Yes, I'll try harder.

Good, you can head down to lunch.

WINK

At lunch things got a bit weird.

Joey looked so cute in gym class today. Did you see?!

Yeah, but I would never go out with a guy who wasn't Hispanic or black.

TOTALLY!

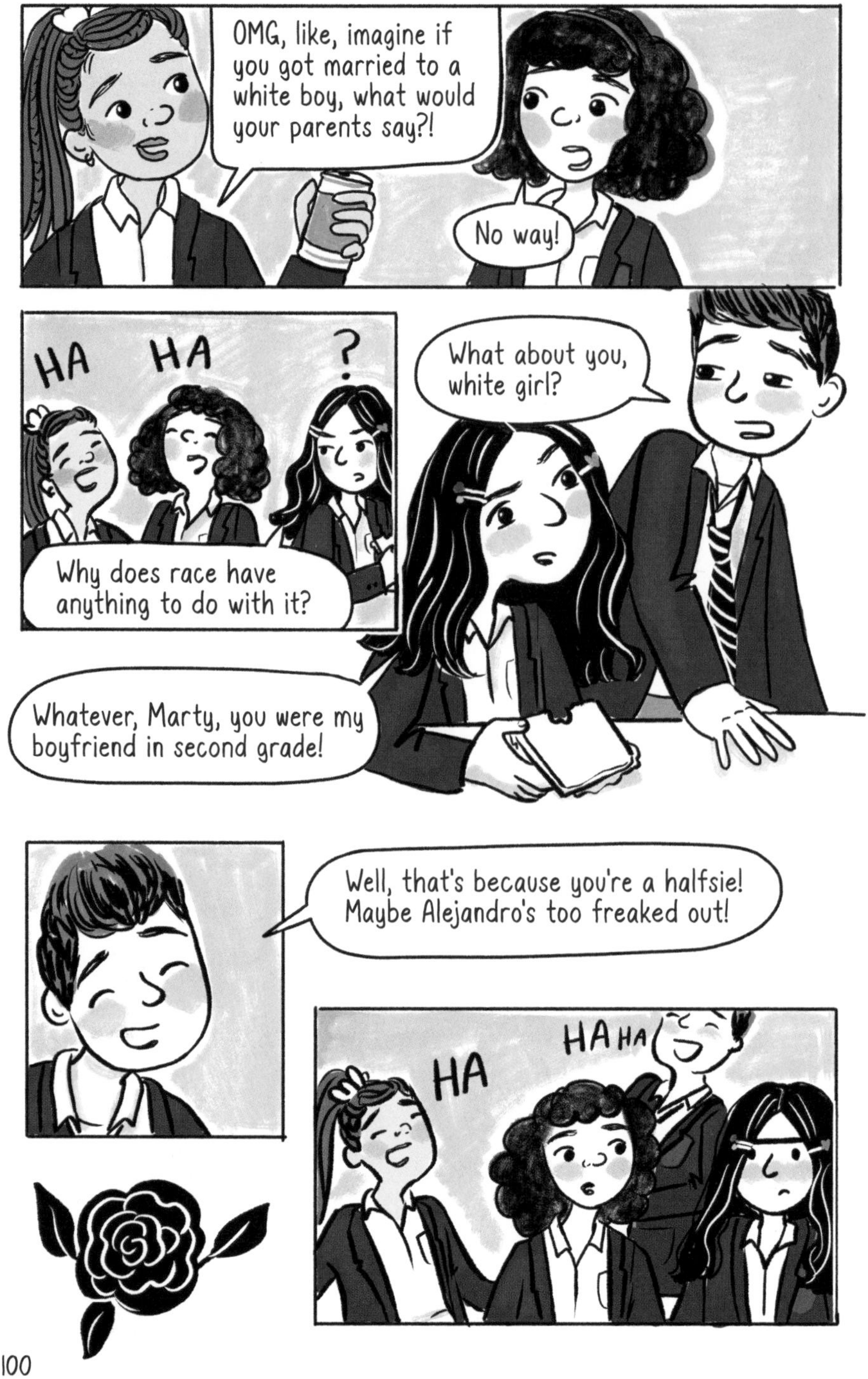
OMG, like, imagine if you got married to a white boy, what would your parents say?!
No way!
HA
HA
?
Why does race have anything to do with it?
What about you, white girl?
Whatever, Marty, you were my boyfriend in second grade!
Well, that's because you're a halfsie! Maybe Alejandro's too freaked out!
HA
HA HA

Sometimes our class feels divided and I don't know which side I am supposed to be on or why there are sides at all. It never seemed to matter before. Now they're always pointing out how I'm only half Puerto Rican. I don't even know if speaking more Spanish will help. It makes me feel like I'm not a whole person.

March 8th, 2001

This weekend I was at Dad's apartment.

We got our Saturday bagels as usual.

DAD: SALT BAGEL NO SPREAD

ME: EVERYTHING BAGEL

VEGGIE CREAM CHEESE

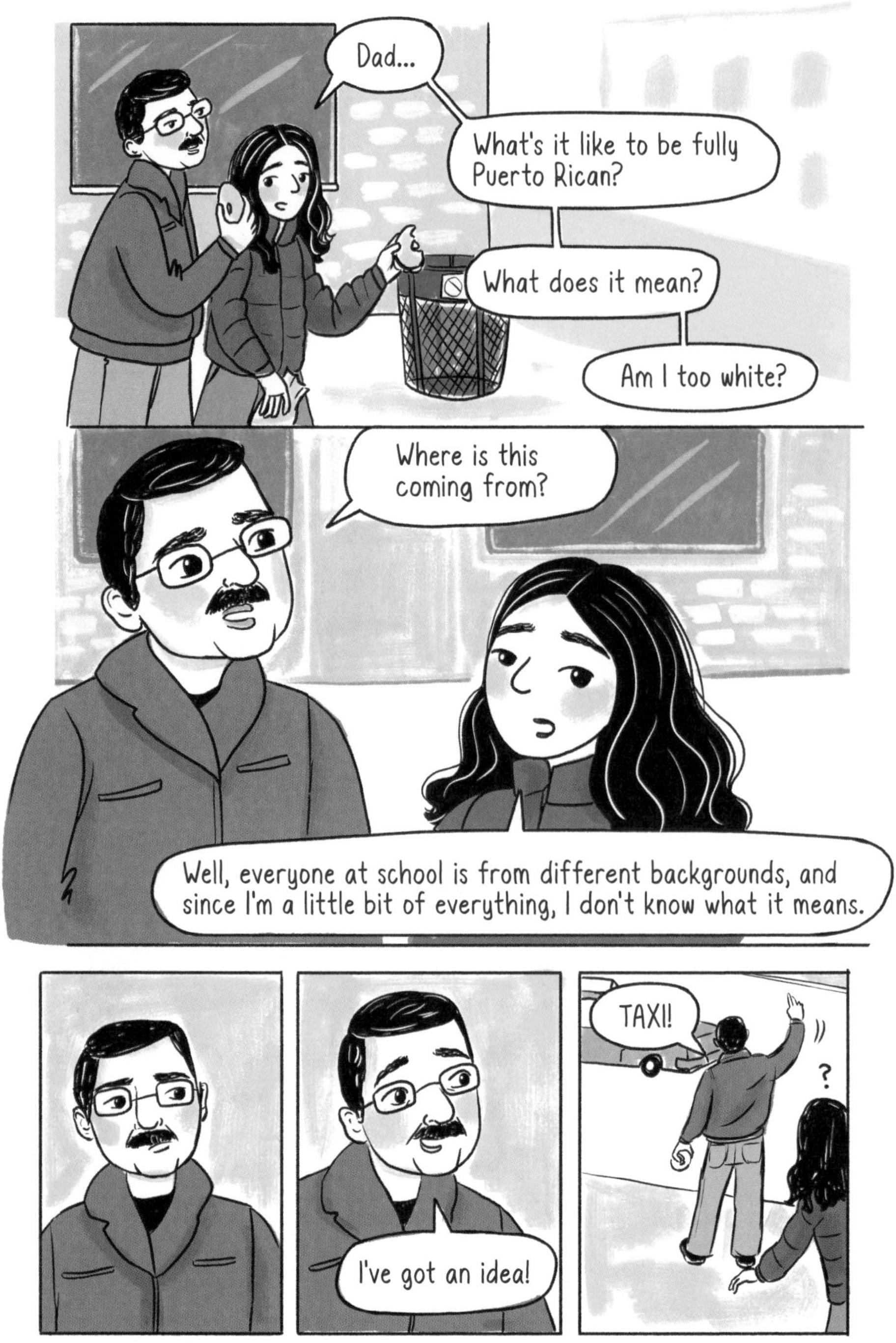

Dad...
What's it like to be fully Puerto Rican?
What does it mean?
Am I too white?
Where is this coming from?
Well, everyone at school is from different backgrounds, and since I'm a little bit of everything, I don't know what it means.
I've got an idea!
TAXI!
?

EL MUSEO
DEL BARRIO
NEW YORK

MUSEUM IS A SCHOOL: THE ARTIST LEARNS TO COMMUNICATE. THE PUBLIC LEARNS TO MAKE CONNECTIONS.

Our ancestors were the Tainos, the native people who lived in Puerto Rico—

—or Borinquen, as they called it.

During the early colonial days there were people from Europe and Africa living there, too.

So our people are from everywhere.

So many artists and musicians in our history, too.

Then Dad bought a Taino cap →

It was sort of confusing because it didn't answer my original question. But it felt nice to be connected, as if our ancestors pulled pieces of interesting things from all over the world and put them together to make me.

Also Puerto Rican

Puerto Rican Haute Couture Fashion!

The next day, Dad remembered the Met classes again for middle school students, so he brought me there to officially start my first class.

ONE OF THE LARGEST MUSEUMS IN THE WORLD!

I was SO nervous at first, but it was actually really cool being around everyone else who liked drawing, too.

It was just an introduction session to start. No one at school appreciates art like I do, so this felt like a whole new world.

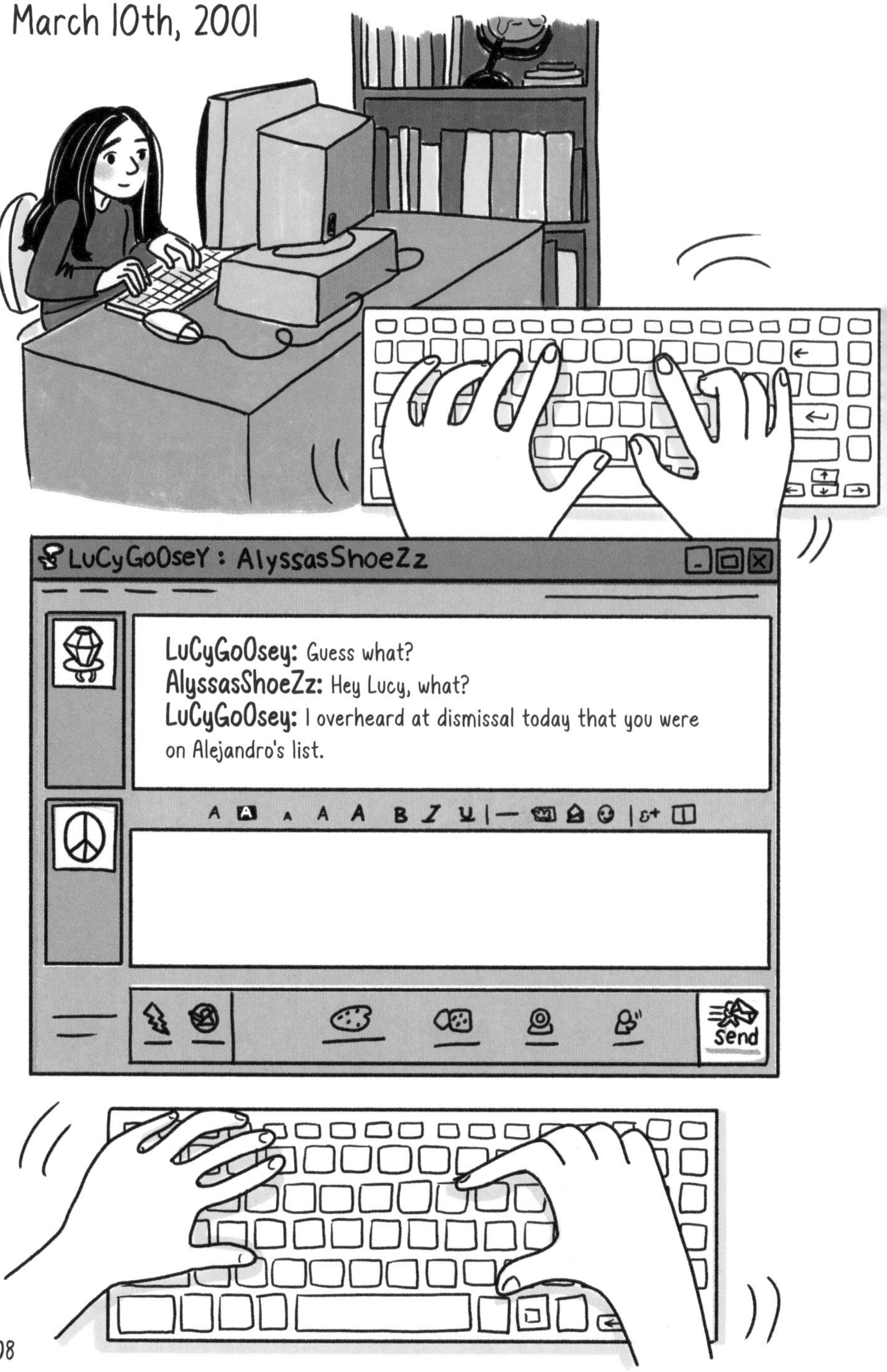
March 10th, 2001
LuCyGoOseY : AlyssasShoeZz
LuCyGoOsey: Guess what?
AlyssasShoeZz: Hey Lucy, what?
LuCyGoOsey: I overheard at dismissal today that you were on Alejandro's list.
Send

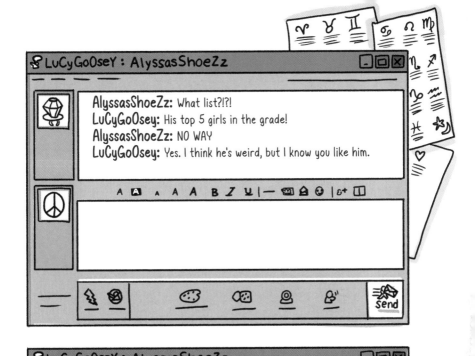

AlyssasShoeZz: What list?!?!
LuCyGoOsey: His top 5 girls in the grade!
AlyssasShoeZz: NO WAY
LuCyGoOsey: Yes. I think he's weird, but I know you like him.

A A A A A B Z U | — 😊 🏠 😊 | 🔒 📖

⚡ 🚫   🎨   🎴   📷   👥   Send

AlyssasShoeZz: Whatever!
LuCyGoOsey: I asked James after if Alejandro was for real or not and he just said, "I'm not saying anything."
AlyssasShoeZz: Whoa. That's pretty close to yes I think.

I thought he just felt bad for me, so the fact that it is even a smidge of a possibility is HUGE. Ten days till Alejandro's birthday. I checked out his horoscope and it said he is most compatible with Taurus, Cancer, AND SCORPIO! (That's ME!) The stars were certainly aligned today.

Dear Alejandro,
HAPPY
BIRTHDAY!
♥
Love,
Alyssa

Dear Diary,

Today was a big shock. When we got to school we were given the terrible news that Sister Marie had a heart attack and died! She wasn't even sick. Now that she's gone, we regret all of the stress we put on her and how we seemed to not care. She just wanted me to be a better student and I was so distracted. I feel so guilty because all she did was try to help. Most of us didn't get a chance to tell her how thankful we were for her.

BE SILENT, AND GO TO YOUR SPECIAL PLACE

Sister Marie was a germaphobe, too, and always sprayed literally everything with Fantastik spray. She once joked with us that she would take Fantastik spray to her grave.

I remember one time she sent a letter home to EACH of my parents about how I had improved with my writing. My parents were so proud. She always brought treats in on the first of the month, too. I can't remember if any of us said thank you and now I feel so guilty.

I think her death made us think a lot more about being kind to people, because you don't know when they'll be gone.

Hopefully she can read my letters in heaven.

Dear Sister
I forgot t
I promise
do better o
tests and ho
I won't let
you down.

- Alys

Dear Sister Marie,
I'm so sorry. I didn't mean to be so bad...
Thank you for always helping me. I'm sorry I didn't listen sometimes...

Yours faithfully,
Alyssa

PS: We all loved you.

Your sorrowful writer,
Alyssa

March 17th, 2001

School classes have resumed with our new teacher, Mr. Sampson. He's been our Latin teacher for three years so he already knows us. The other teachers, including the principal, are covering the rest of the classes that Sister Marie usually taught, like English, Religion, and Social Studies. Our class agreed to keep the tradition of bringing in treats on the first of the month to remember how special she was to us. It feels like things can change in the blink of an eye. It kind of scares me.

March 23rd, 2001

Today, instead of walking straight to Dad's apartment, I took a much longer route home. Things are getting as normal as they can be at school, but I just have so many feelings swirling around in my head! I'm worried about the future and all of the elements I can't control.

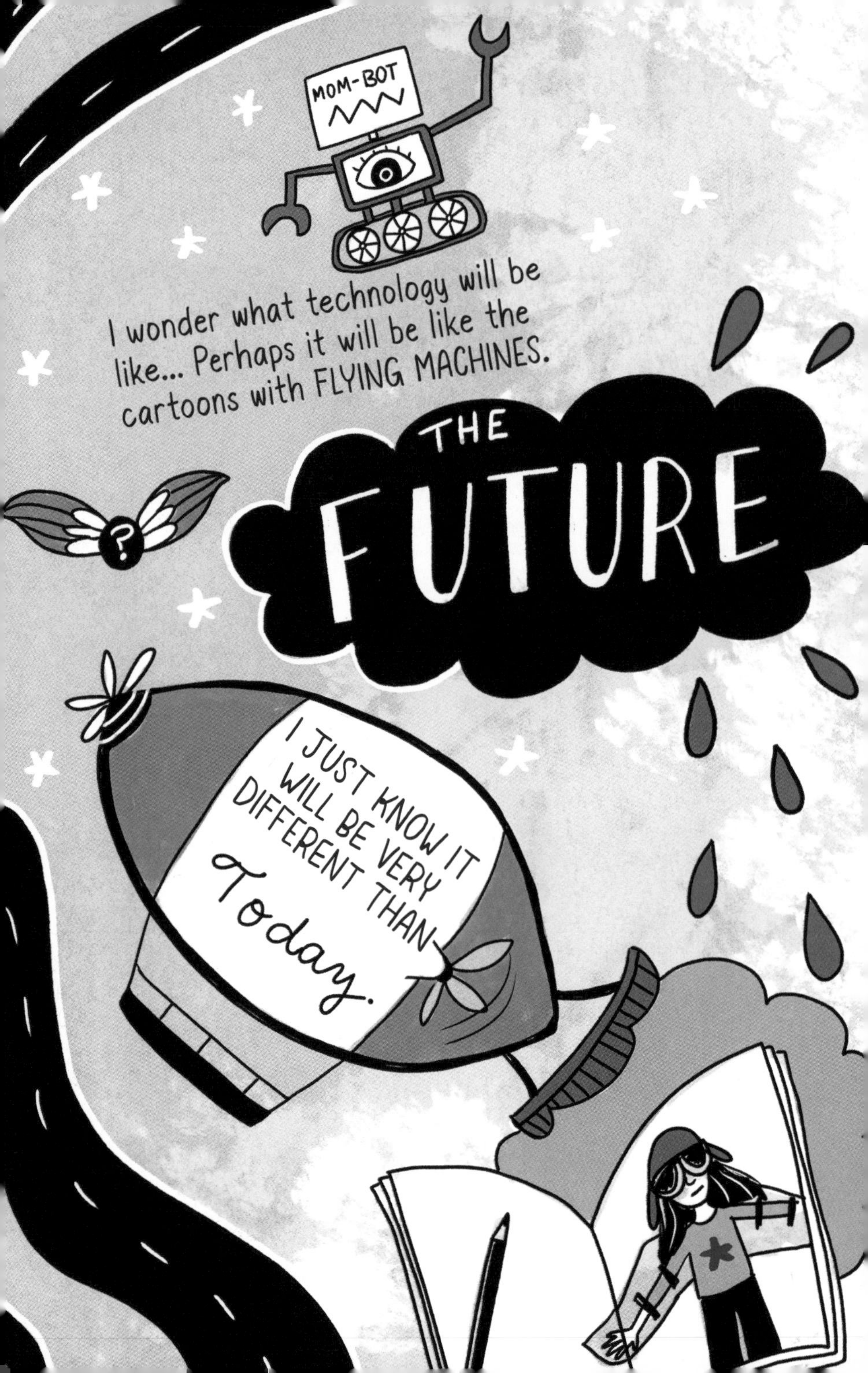
MOM-BOT
I wonder what technology will be like... Perhaps it will be like the cartoons with FLYING MACHINES.
THE FUTURE
I JUST KNOW IT WILL BE VERY DIFFERENT THAN Today.

Luckily, art class seemed to help.

And when I got home, I just wanted to be by myself.

April 9th, 2001

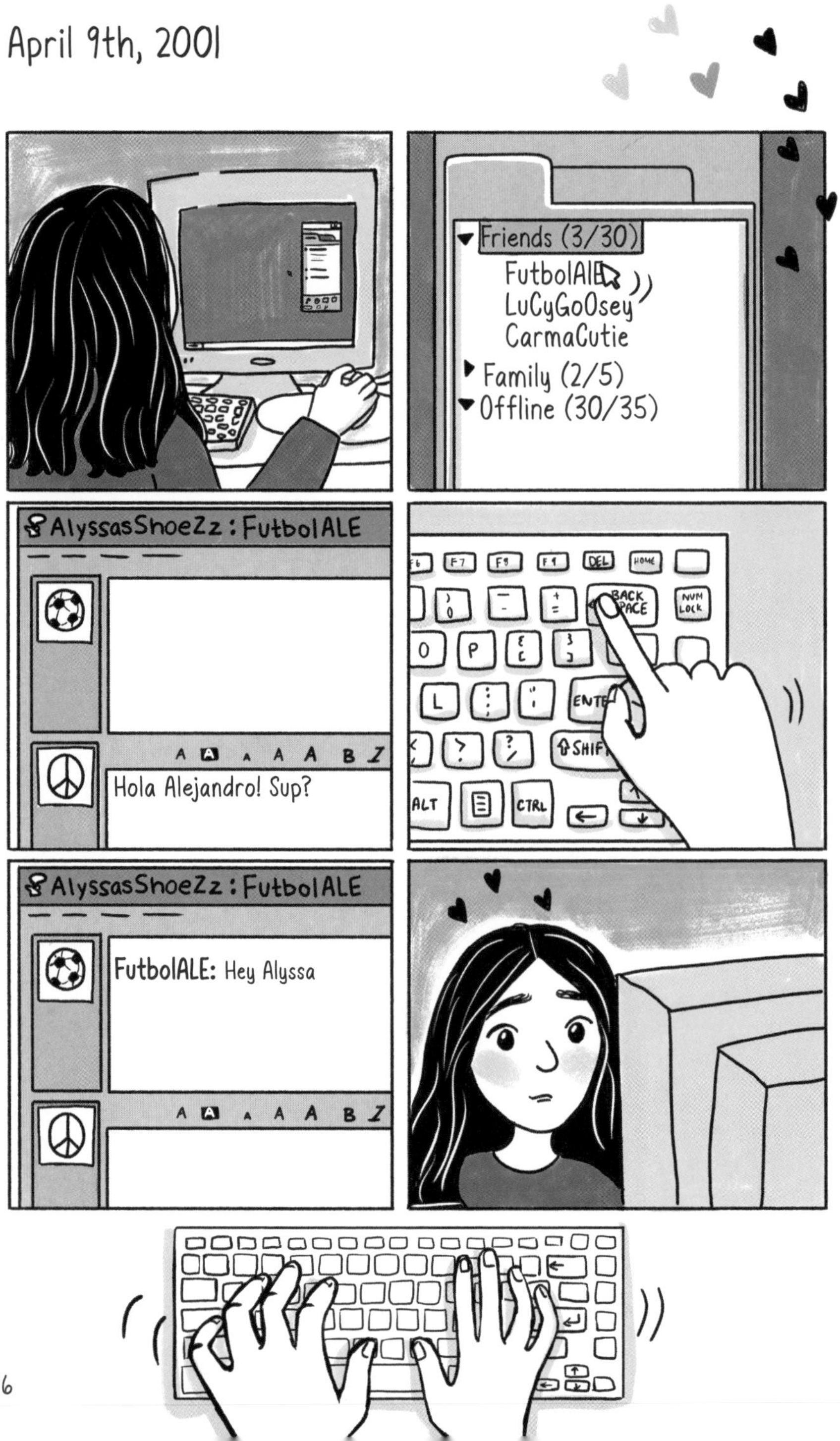
Friends (3/30)
FutbolALE
LuCyGoOsey
CarmaCutie
Family (2/5)
Offline (30/35)
AlyssasShoeZz : FutbolALE
Hola Alejandro! Sup?
AlyssasShoeZz : FutbolALE
FutbolALE: Hey Alyssa

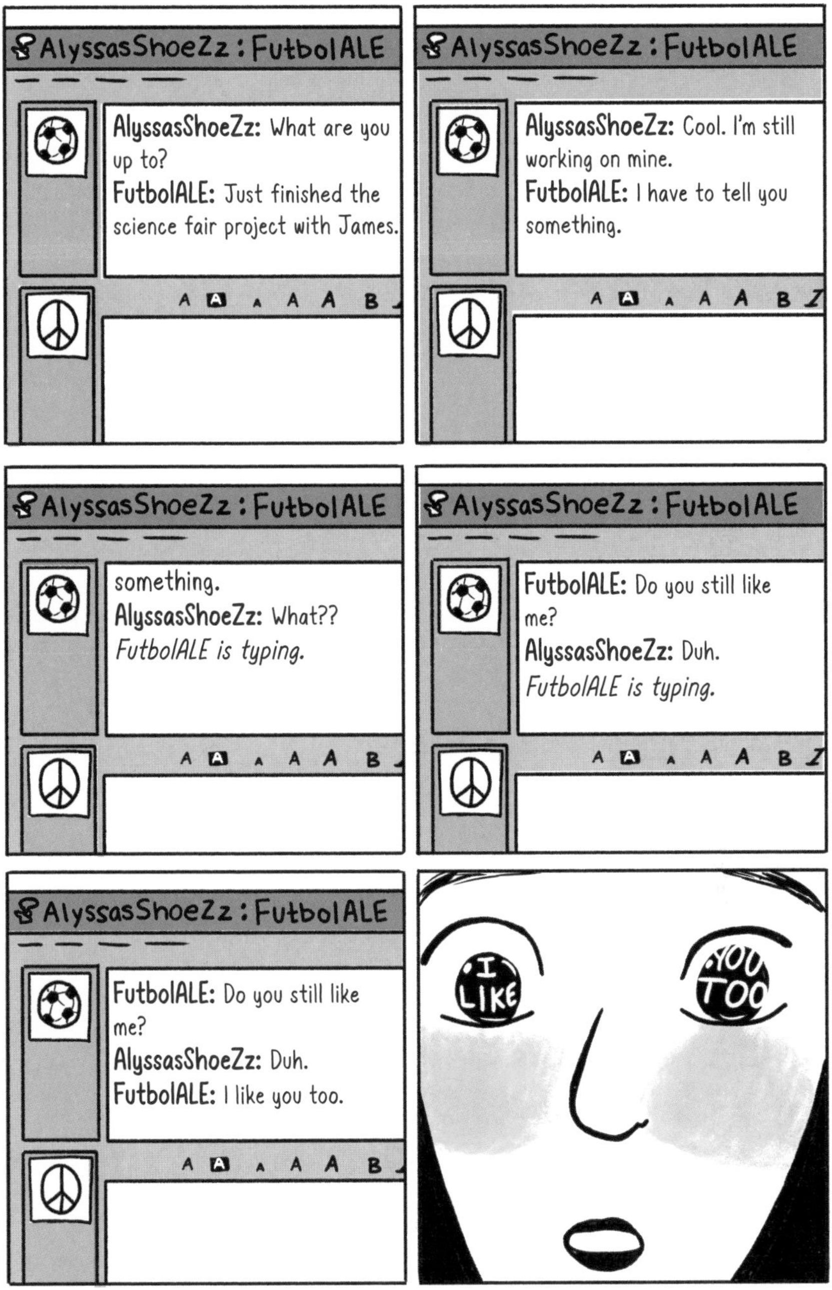
AlyssasShoeZz : FutbolALE
AlyssasShoeZz: What are you up to?
FutbolALE: Just finished the science fair project with James.
AlyssasShoeZz : FutbolALE
AlyssasShoeZz: Cool. I'm still working on mine.
FutbolALE: I have to tell you something.
AlyssasShoeZz : FutbolALE
something.
AlyssasShoeZz: What??
FutbolALE is typing.
AlyssasShoeZz : FutbolALE
FutbolALE: Do you still like me?
AlyssasShoeZz: Duh.
FutbolALE is typing.
AlyssasShoeZz : FutbolALE
FutbolALE: Do you still like me?
AlyssasShoeZz: Duh.
FutbolALE: I like you too.
I LIKE
YOU TOO

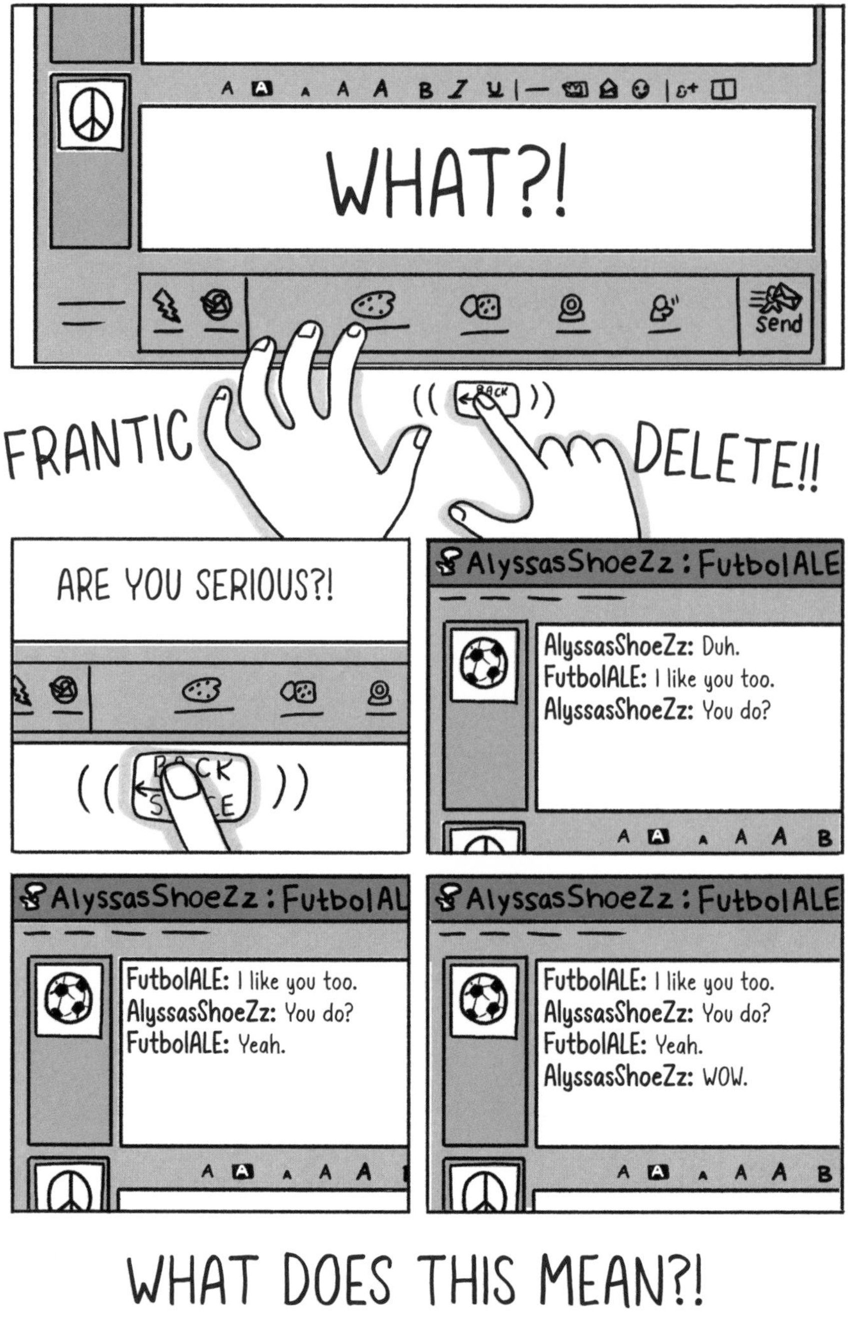
WHAT?!
send
BACK
FRANTIC DELETE!!
ARE YOU SERIOUS?!
BACK SPACE
AlyssasShoeZz : FutbolALE
AlyssasShoeZz: Duh.
FutbolALE: I like you too.
AlyssasShoeZz: You do?
AlyssasShoeZz : FutbolAL
FutbolALE: I like you too.
AlyssasShoeZz: You do?
FutbolALE: Yeah.
AlyssasShoeZz : FutbolALE
FutbolALE: I like you too.
AlyssasShoeZz: You do?
FutbolALE: Yeah.
AlyssasShoeZz: WOW.
WHAT DOES THIS MEAN?!

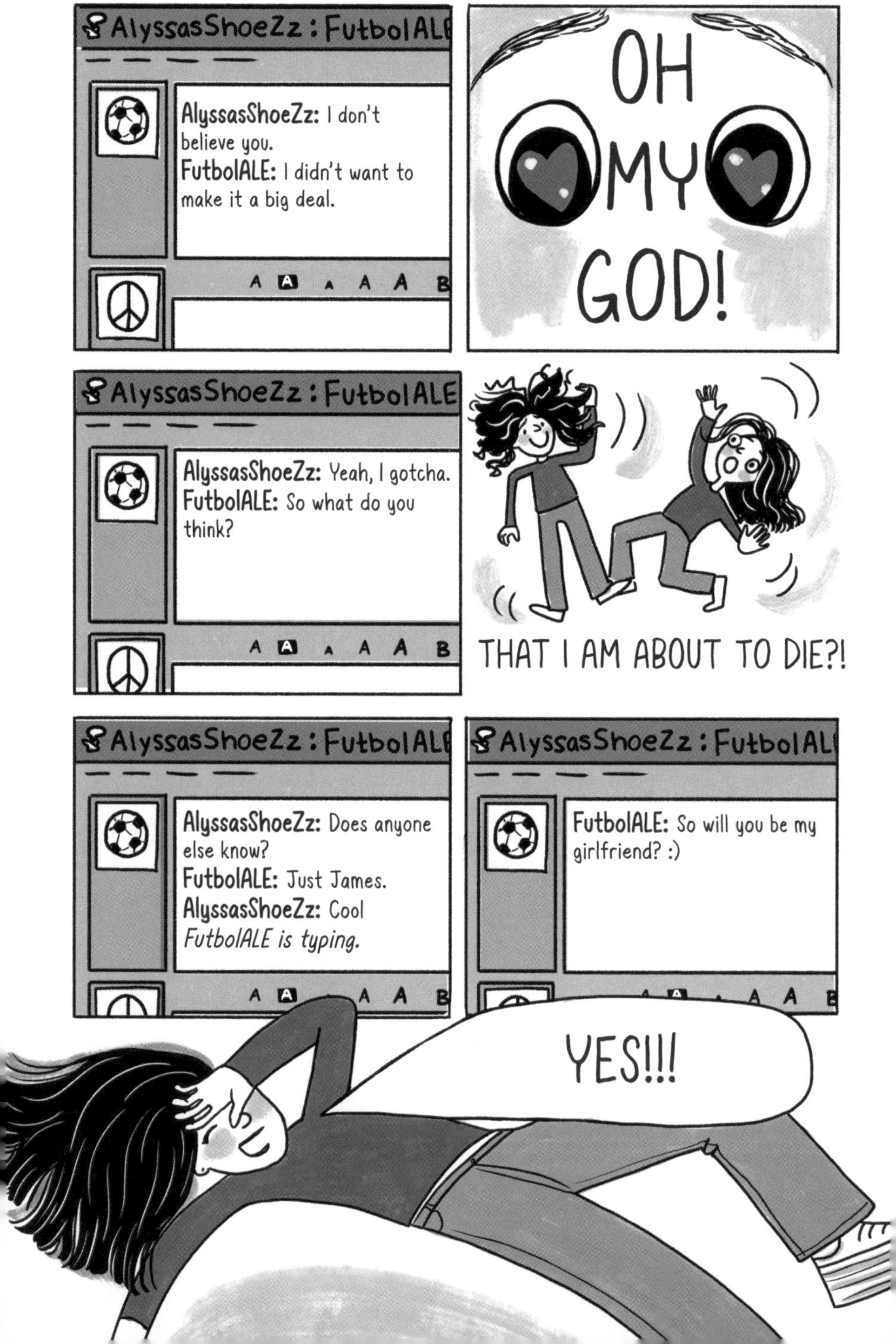
AlyssasShoeZz : FutbolALE
AlyssasShoeZz: I don't believe you.
FutbolALE: I didn't want to make it a big deal.
A A A A A B
OH MY GOD!
AlyssasShoeZz : FutbolALE
AlyssasShoeZz: Yeah, I gotcha.
FutbolALE: So what do you think?
A A A A A B
THAT I AM ABOUT TO DIE?!
AlyssasShoeZz : FutbolALE
AlyssasShoeZz: Does anyone else know?
FutbolALE: Just James.
AlyssasShoeZz: Cool
FutbolALE is typing.
AlyssasShoeZz : FutbolALE
FutbolALE: So will you be my girlfriend? :)
YES!!!

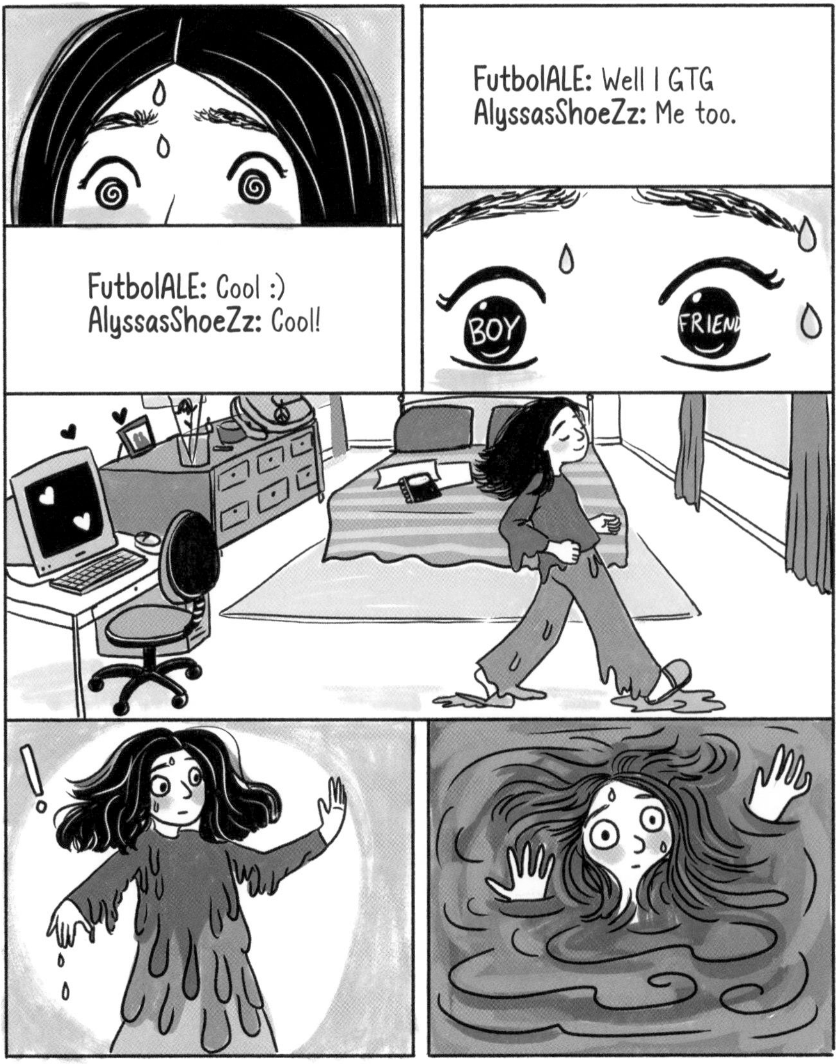
FutbolALE: Well I GTG
AlyssasShoeZz: Me too.
FutbolALE: Cool :)
AlyssasShoeZz: Cool!
BOY
FRIEND

What if he's not serious?!

April 10th, 2001

Alejandro is my BOYFRIEND. After quickly confirming with him that it was NOT a joke and that it was actually him typing those words to me, I spent the rest of the day in a distracted haze of butterflies and near-barf experiences.

Everyone at school is already so annoying about it. Maybe if everyone didn't make fun of us, Alejandro would be able to act like himself and not hide who he really is. I need to work on that myself, too.

April 12th, 2001

Today was science presentation day at school, but more importantly, I spent one-on-one time with Alejandro! I was about to get pizza with Lucy and Carmen when Alejandro came over to ask me if he could walk me home.

We talked about the science fair and how long it took to work on it.

And then James appeared.

Oh, hey! You guys walking this way, too?

Can you believe how much homework we have this week?!

Blah blah blah

Blah blah

Oh! That's me. See you tomorrow!

78ᵗʰ Street

Finally...

Well, you should probably walk to your house now, because if my neighbors or the doorman see me being walked home by a boy, they will FREAK OUT.

Oh. Yeah, that makes sense.

I'm going to my mom's later when she gets out of work. I could call you...

Yeah, that sounds good.

Okay...bye!

Bye!

Mom said I'm too young for a boyfriend, but as long as the walks home are the only "date" we have that it's okay. She also told me to not call him too much because he's so shy, he might get overwhelmed. I will try my best, but it's so hard to resist!

April 14th, 2001

As this pen hits the paper I am proud to announce that my unibrow situation is over. Mom brought me to her salon today.

Side note: I looked straight into Alejandro's face yesterday and noticed he had a little goatee. How weird!

April 15th, 2001

Happy Easter! I feel so guilty and conflicted.

If my parents or teachers knew how distracted I was, they would be so disappointed. It's like I know that it's wrong, but I am letting myself go crazy anyway!

Dad and I rode our bikes home from church. It was like the Alejandro tour.

That's where he looked me in the eyes.

That's where we parted ways.

April 17th, 2001

I guess not much has actually changed with Alejandro being my boyfriend. We just talk a little bit more now. But it's still A DREAM!

After our phone call it was time to get to work!

With just a few months until we are in eighth grade, I'm starting to freak out about high school options. Carmen and I joked around that we are going to literally turn into giant index cards with the amount of notes we are taking for finals.

With high schools looking at every detail, I CANNOT end up with a low average. My parents want me to apply to schools in Queens, but none of my friends will be there. Carmen wants me to apply to Dominican Academy so that we can be together. I'm not sure what I really want. I wondered where Alejandro wanted to go, so I asked him, too.

May 4th, 2001

I tried to find out a little more about Alejandro today: What he wants to be when he grows up, what he likes to do, etc. So far all I've really learned is that he likes soccer, his favorite subject is Math, and he doesn't like pasta. He just sort of changes the topic to homework. How can he not like pasta, though?! I'll have to forgive him, I guess.

Next week everyone is going to Central Park after school for a water fight. I begged Mom to go, and after a lot of arguing, she's agreed to push my arrival time to Dad's until 5:30 PM! I am never allowed to go to ANYTHING and I'm so excited.

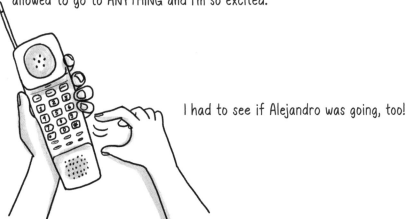

I had to see if Alejandro was going, too!

Yeah, I was just eating some mac and cheese.

• • •

Cool.

• • •

What did you do after school?

• • •

I played soccer with my brother and then just studied.

Are you going to the water fight next week?

• • •

What water fight?

Everyone is going! You should come.

• • •

Okay, I'll see if I can.

May 10th, 2001

Art class this weekend was really neat. We sketched some of the pottery with mythological scenes in the museum and then came up with our own stories on ceramics. Some of the other kids had REALLY cool ideas like elephant characters decorating giant vases or the elderly rain god as a wrinkly cloud.

FRENCH 1780s shoes

INDIAN 19TH-Century SHOE:

They were so creative! When I got back to Mom's place I sketched until my arm hurt. I wanted to tell Alejandro about it, too, but he doesn't really like art.

May 11th, 2001

I've had a very strange thought today. What do I actually even like about Alejandro? Now that he's actually my boyfriend, I'm not fully sure anymore. Do we have anything in common? Does it matter?

In an alternate universe we would both be outgoing, funny, and charming like the couples in movies.

May 13th, 2001

Today was a cursed day. Cursed! After school we got ready for the water fight.

I knew my luck wouldn't last...

Yo, Alyssa! I'm surprised to even see you outside school. You not grounded for once?

Whatever, keep walking.

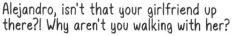

Alejandro, isn't that your girlfriend up there?! Why aren't you walking with her?

We all took off our shoes as soon as we got to the field area.
Everyone immediately went NUTS.

Carmen and I checked the time while we filled up some more balloons. It was 4:45, which was perfect! That meant I had about fifteen minutes left with enough time to get to my dad's place by 5:30. We came up with our grand plan to attack Lucy with our last balloon batch.

In the basketball courts we found Lucy and launched our last ones at her.

And that's when the real disaster began.

We scanned the whole area and the shoes were nowhere in sight.
(Thank goodness I wasn't wearing my prized platforms...)

We retraced our steps and finally found our hidden shoes near a bench.

Before I knew it, in my horrified state I couldn't find my way out of the park. After circling around, I eventually saw our usual exit. I didn't know what time it was anymore, but I knew it was BAD. By the time I frantically ran into the building and through the door, it was too late. I could practically see the steam coming out of the phone.

She thinks I have no respect and don't appreciate what they do for me. I feel so misunderstood! Sometimes I have bad days. I meant it when I said I was sorry. I'm not ungrateful! Sometimes you just can't win.

May 14th, 2001

Still grounded?

Always.

Haha..

Maybe when I'm older I will finally not be grounded for life.

Mm-hmm...

. . .

I think my mom needed me to help her with something before bed.

I'll see you tomorrow, Alejandro!

Okay, yeah, see you tomorrow.

Oh, my god, I can't believe I did that. My mom didn't really need anything! It was so brave of him to call me and it was finally just us on the phone without anyone pushing or shoving us around to talk. Why did I do that?!

your confused writer,
alyssa

May 15th, 2001

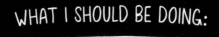
WHAT I SHOULD BE DOING:

WHAT I AM ACTUALLY DOING:

snow boots

cowboy boots

rain boots

hiking boots

party boots

May 20th, 2001

Things that would make the future brighter:

- 365 pairs of shoes. One for each day.
- Becoming a super genius.
- An available cure for all diseases.
- Robot friends.
- Time machines to go back to when things were easier.
- Figuring out how to tell Alejandro the truth...

May 26th, 2001

I'm not sure what has come over me in the midst of my sorrowful week, but I think I've realized that having Alejandro as a boyfriend isn't exactly what I expected it to be. Liking him from afar let my imagination take over beyond reality. All I wanted was for him to like me back.

I went to join Mom watching TV and she could tell something was off. Her All-Seeing Eye can see inside, too.

I had not been able to say the words out loud yet.

June 1st, 2001

Finals are finally over, but the situation at school is NOT any easier.

I think we'll be in Colombia for most of it.

Oh, cool! Do you still have lots of friends there?

Sort of...

I think I'm going on a trip with my dad. Only if my grades are good enough, though...

...

Hey, Alejandro...

I was thinking

and I think

I mean I believe

with summer coming and—

—and everything that's been going on...

That maybe we should go back to being just friends.

Oh...wow.

I sort of wish things were a bit different.

Yeah, me, too.

I'm really sorry.

Yeah, well, I should go.

When I got to Dad's he looked a bit off. He said he was home sick after a doctor's appointment. I told him it was the worst day and I'm pretty sure he thought I was talking about finals.

I haven't told a soul yet. I just feel so lonely and guilty. No one would understand at school and I can't talk about it with my parents. I hope Alejandro doesn't hate me forever. Since Dad looked a bit sad, too, I called Mom to see if I could just stay the night here. She agreed that it was a good idea if Dad wasn't well. It was reassuring to hear that even though they are broken up, it's possible to still be friends sometimes.

June 10th, 2001

Well, I did better than I thought on finals, so that's one layer of relief.

The school fair is this week, and we are pretty much done with all important schoolwork by this point.

Have you talked to Alejandro much?

A little, but I think he's avoiding me.

I think he REALLY liked you. You definitely broke his heart.

Summer 2001

Mom made me organize everything in sight today. She said now that it's summer vacation I should do more around the house to help her. It's not that I don't want to help her, she just gets so crazy about it!

I think Dad is lonely. He asked me if I would be okay with him dating. I guess I am okay with it. I just don't want him to be sad...and I don't want him to spend less time with me because it's always just the two of us.

Europe is too far and my backpack is too small to bring this diary, so I've decided to leave it at home and just do my writing to Mom in postcards! Ciao, diary!

Your traveling writer,
Alyssa

Dear Mom, today we went to the Uffizi Gallery and saw some really amazing paintings. I also bought an umbrella with the same chubby baby angel painting as this postcard. It's been raining like crazy! We had the most delicious pasta ever yesterday and because it was so good, we decided to go again today to order the same thing! You would've LOVED it.

Linda Martin
123 45th Street
Forest Hills, NY 11375
USA

Hi, Mom! My feet are about to fall off from walking so much. Good thing Dad speaks Italian because we got lost! I made a wish at the Trevi Fountain and also found a little present for you. Everyone rides motorcycles here! Sometimes you see people riding with their dogs on board, too!

Linda Martin
123 45th Street
Forest Hills, NY 11375
USA

Momster, this whole city smells
a bit funny. It was too expensive
to do a gondola ride, so instead
we walked around and looked
in all of the little shops with
masks.

Linda Martin
123 45th Street
Forest Hills, NY 11375
USA

Dear Mom! We had a crazy day
when we accidentally took an
express train. Dad does NOT
speak French so it took a lot
longer to figure out. Tomorrow
we are going to the Louvre
and will see the Mona Lisa. I've
already used up all of the film
in my camera so hopefully I can
buy another one somewhere.

Linda Martin
123 45th Street
Forest Hills, NY 11375

USA

Hey, Mom! I tasted some of Dad's cappuccino today. It's funny how all of the people in Paris face their cafe chairs out to the street. It makes it easier to check out all of the funky outfits and shoes walking by!

Linda Martin
123 45th Street
Forest Hills, NY 11375
USA

Hi, Mom!
It's me again! Remember me? It feels like I've been gone forever. I can't wait to wear my regular clothes instead of washing and wearing my same stuff every day. Dad ordered SNAILS to eat, which was pretty funny. I just couldn't do it!

Linda Martin
123 45th Street
Forest Hills, NY 11375
USA

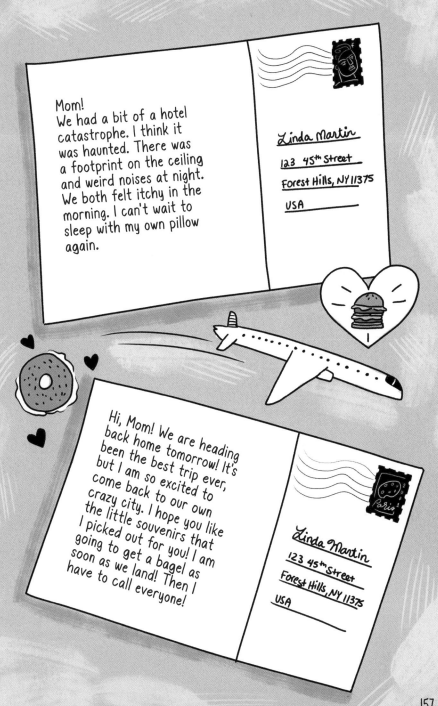

Mom!
We had a bit of a hotel catastrophe. I think it was haunted. There was a footprint on the ceiling and weird noises at night. We both felt itchy in the morning. I can't wait to sleep with my own pillow again.

Linda Martin
123 45th Street
Forest Hills, NY 11375
USA

Hi, Mom! We are heading back home tomorrow! It's been the best trip ever, but I am so excited to come back to our own crazy city. I hope you like the little souvenirs that I picked out for you! I am going to get a bagel as soon as we land! Then I have to call everyone!

Linda Martin
123 45th Street
Forest Hills, NY 11375
USA

Dear Diary,

It's me again! I can't believe summer is over and I have to go back to black-loafer life soon. I've at least managed to find the highest heeled ones that school will allow.

SCHOOL SHOES

When Dad and I were away, we walked ALL DAY everywhere so I was pretty relieved to be wearing sneakers. I can still picture the glamorous people sipping coffee on the sidewalks in Rome and Paris. We also saw so many artists drawing outdoors and sketching in museums. It reminded me of my art classes at the Met, but times a million. I especially loved a painting called *Primavera* by Botticelli. It reminds me of a fashion show from another time and world.

I'm having mixed feelings about eighth grade. In one way I'm excited to see my friends and have a fresh start with a new me. But I'm also a bit scared of getting into high school next year. I think I'm ready, but I don't want to let anyone down. And hopefully everything on the Alejandro front is okay. I'm sure we can be friends, but I'm scared he hates me now.

September 3rd, 2001

School starts this week! Carmen, Lucy, and I are in the same class, too! We decided to do some accessory shopping to change up our looks.

September 5th, 2001

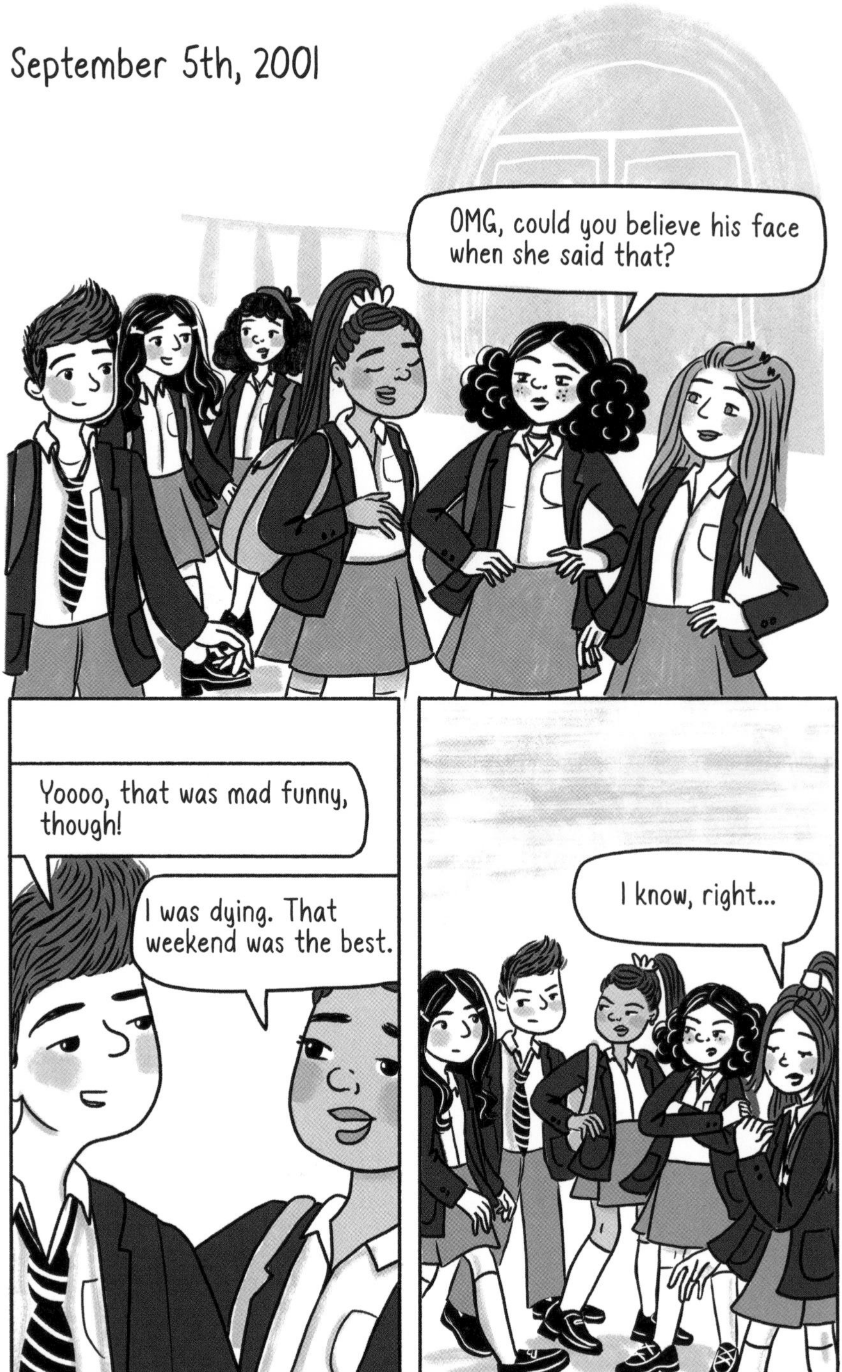
OMG, could you believe his face when she said that?
Yoooo, that was mad funny, though!
I was dying. That weekend was the best.
I know, right...

Here we go again. The popularity contest is back.

Alphabetic seating, everyone!

I looked around to see where Alejandro was. I hoped that he wasn't still mad at me.

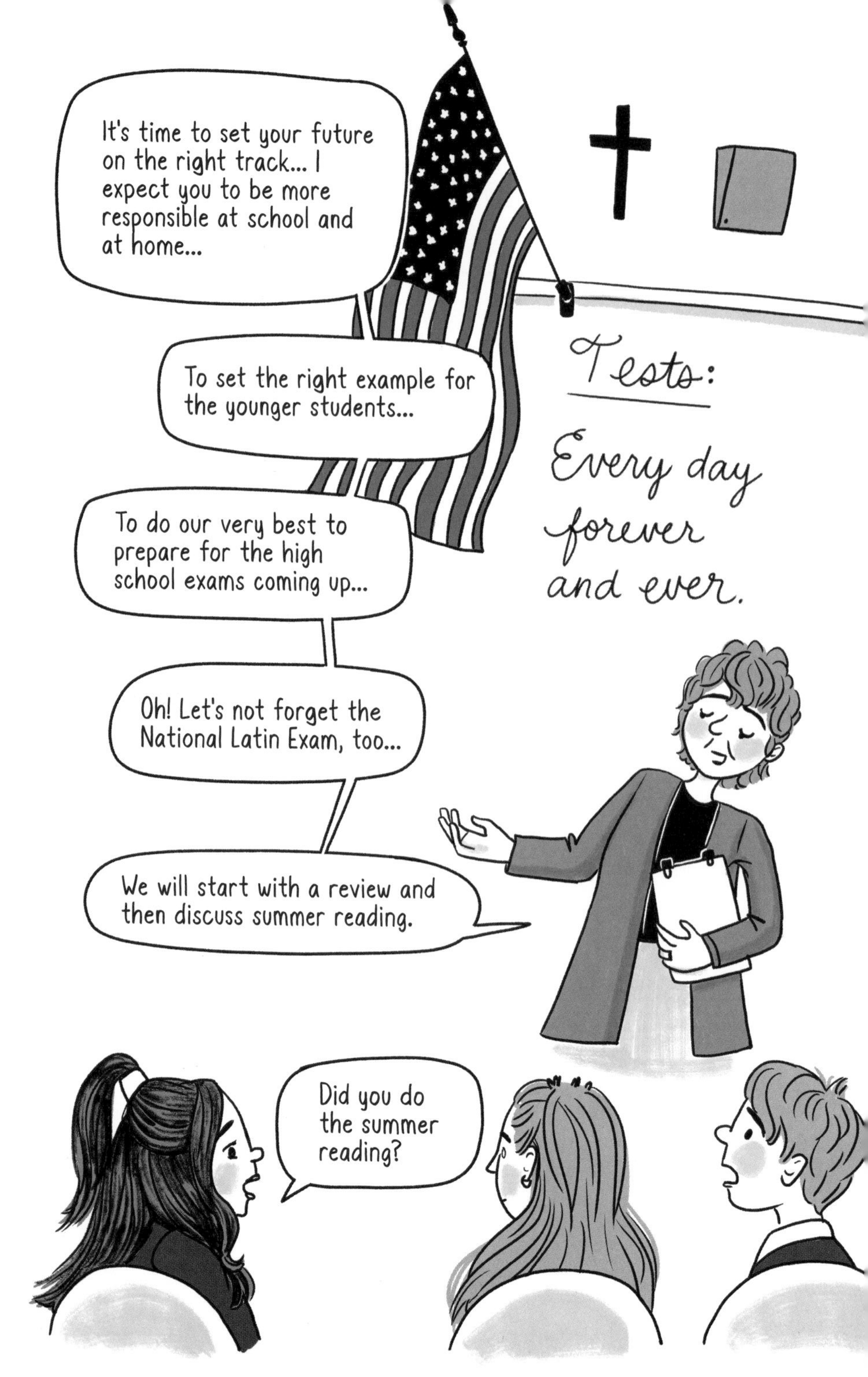
It's time to set your future on the right track... I expect you to be more responsible at school and at home...
Tests:
Every day forever and ever.
To set the right example for the younger students...
To do our very best to prepare for the high school exams coming up...
Oh! Let's not forget the National Latin Exam, too...
We will start with a review and then discuss summer reading.
Did you do the summer reading?

Today when I got home from the first full day back, I just collapsed into a pile of high expectations and misery from having so many zits at the beginning of the school year.

In an alternative universe...I would be a zit-free fashion designer with a shoe for every day, strutting confidently like the ladies in Europe. Everyone would want to be my friend and my mysteriously long eyelashes would brush away all of the mean people.

The good news is that my parents agreed to let me go to Dad's after school like usual or take the subway home to my mom's house the whole way by myself. I can't go another year being a complete loser. I'll be thirteen in two months!

September 7th, 2001

Why does gym class have to be the worst?!

Dumbass probably still can't speak English after all this time.

YOU'RE the dumbass!

Ohhhh, Alyssa, protecting lover boy still?

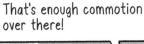

It's like the boys will do or say anything for attention. And everyone just laughs along with them! I spent most of the day coming up with new comebacks that I would never have the guts to say out loud. None of them were any good... I honestly do not know how anyone survives middle school. Is there a kit that you can buy?

September 11th, 2001

~~Today...~~

September 12th, 2001

~~Yesterday...~~

September 13th, 2001

I don't even know how to say it...

September 14th, 2001

I haven't been able to write anything yet. Here's what happened on the 11th. We were in first period English class just like any other day.

The teachers had very serious faces, so we knew whatever this was about was different. We wondered what could be so important.

I hope this means we don't have to take that summer reading quiz!

I bet someone cheated and we can't leave until someone fesses up!

Why would they bring seventh graders to that, too?!

Ohh, yeah... I dunno, then.

We walked into the auditorium, but there were no seats set up.

So our teacher led us to the church instead.

We've brought you here to announce some very serious news that we have just received.

Earlier this morning a plane crashed into one of the twin tower buildings downtown.

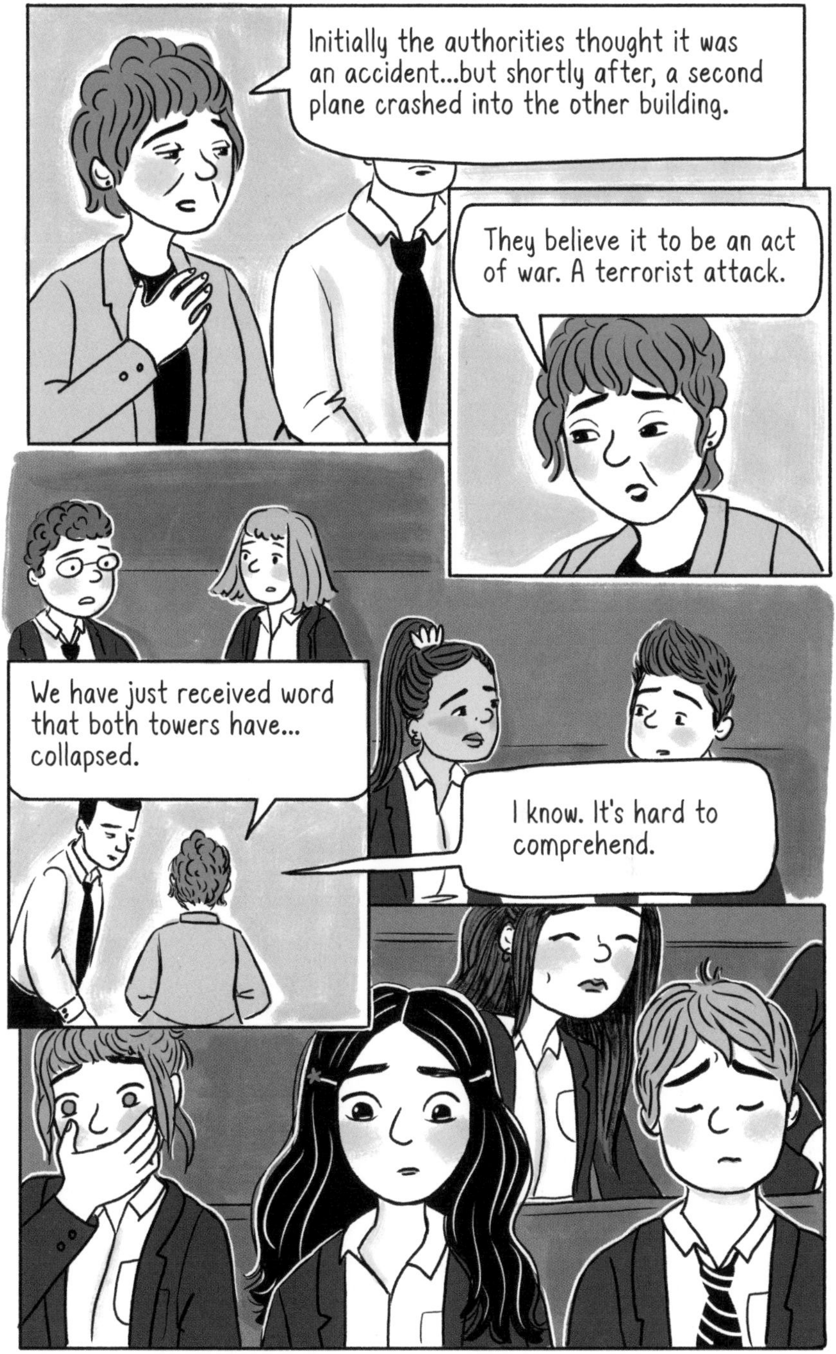
Initially the authorities thought it was an accident...but shortly after, a second plane crashed into the other building.
They believe it to be an act of war. A terrorist attack.
We have just received word that both towers have... collapsed.
I know. It's hard to comprehend.

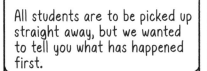

All students are to be picked up straight away, but we wanted to tell you what has happened first.

We don't know any more yet. The younger students will be told by their families when they get picked up.

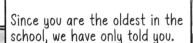

Since you are the oldest in the school, we have only told you.

We know that many of your families work in that area, and the office is getting in touch with them right now.

Before we head back in to pack up, let us pray.

Dear God. Don't let anything happen to my parents. Please.

No one was allowed to leave the school without a parent, not even eighth graders. Some students were picked up immediately.

What's a terrorist attack?

I played the timeline in my head over and over again.

If Mom starts work at 8:30 and Dad starts work at 9, maybe they are fine.

But wait...if Mom got to work late... or...

...Dad went bike riding instead? Still fine, right?

Or maybe they were there and didn't get away in time...

No, no. That's not possible...

Nice! Well, this means I'm going home to play video games.

Dude, this is, like, really serious.

I was joking, duh...

You can't joke about this. What's your problem?!

More and more names were announced over the loudspeaker and more students gradually left.

I'll call you later.

I waited there for hours with no news. No nothing. Finally the last few of us were sent downstairs to wait near the office.

And then it was just me. The last one in the school.

The school secretary finally came up to me with a look of relief.

Both Mom and Dad are fine, but can't get here with the whole city shut down.

I've spoken to your mom and she says we can all wait for your dad to get home at our place.

The subways aren't running, but your mom got to Queens in time. She knows you're coming with us.

Do you smell that?

It sort of smells like burnt grilled cheese.

You can see smoke from the terrace.

I wondered if my parents had to run like that...

Let's just turn this off for a little while. Alyss, you'll be with your dad soon—

KNOCK
KNOCK
KNOCK

I was so relieved that my parents were okay, and even more so when I saw them. Later that day I asked them what it had been like that morning.

Dad started his day as he usually does—riding down the bike path to the Financial District.

Mom and Dad work here.

8:25 AM

But Dad had to meet new clients in Jersey City, so he didn't have to be in the World Trade Center that morning. He hopped on the PATH train.

ABOUT 1/2 MILE

8:40 AM

Mom was at her desk already. Her office faced the Twin Towers.

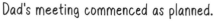
Dad's meeting commenced as planned.

Until they saw something unusual outside...

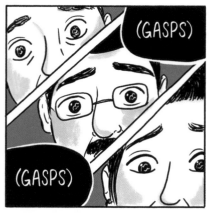

They tried to keep everyone calm at Mom's office.

Mom knew something wasn't right, though.

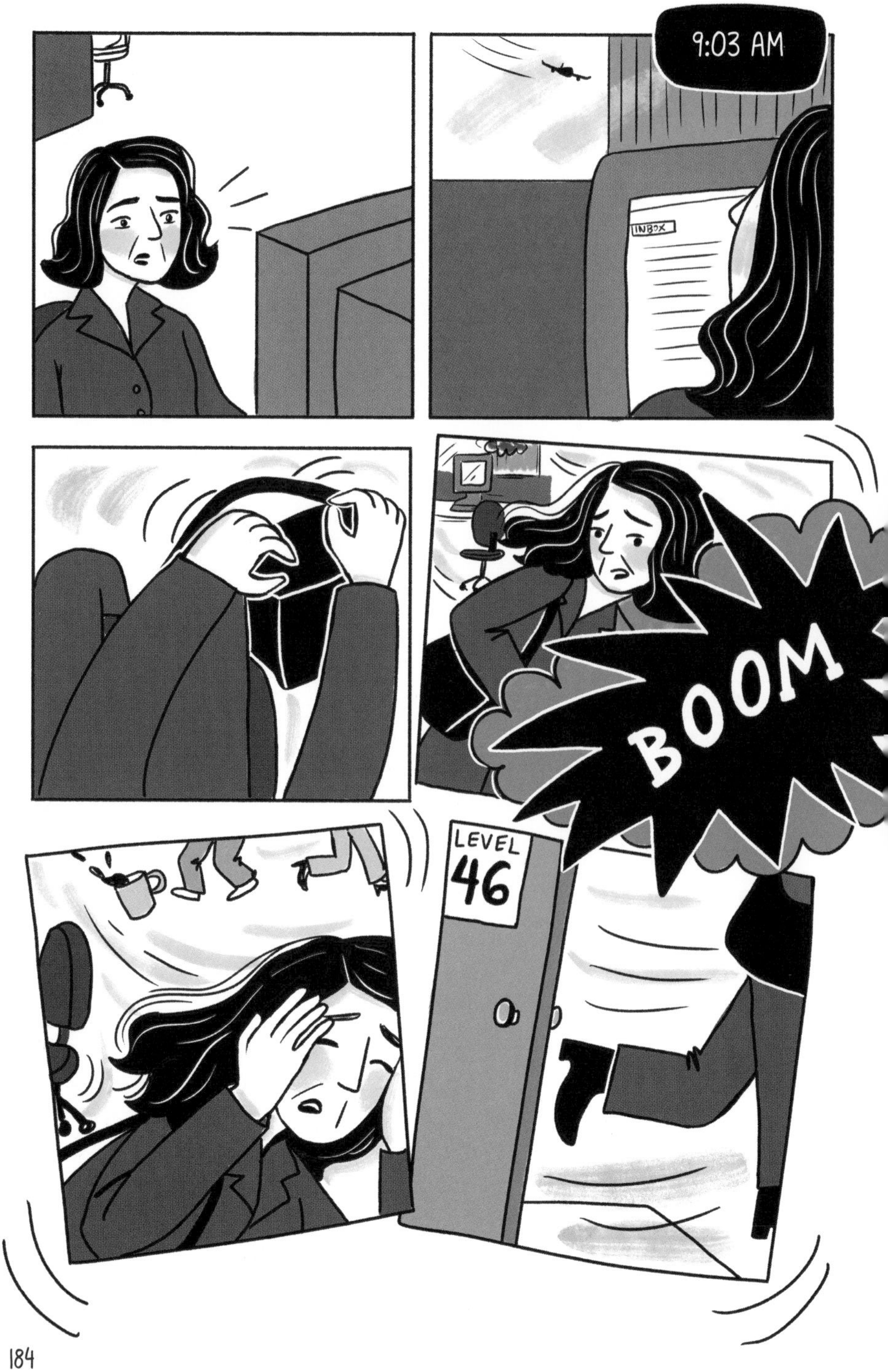
9:03 AM
INBOX
BOOM
LEVEL
46

They couldn't believe their eyes as an orange flash erupted from the second tower.

9:04 AM

A second plane!

Dad ran out without his briefcase.

Mom kept running.

PANT PANT

When Dad got to the station, he was stopped by an officer.

The PATH train is shut down and only emergency vehicles are allowed into lower Manhattan.

What about the ferry?

Sorry.

There was no way back from there, so he came up with a plan B.

Is there a bike shop around here?

Nah, not in this area, but there's a skate shop over on Monmouth Street.

Thanks.

Mom must have been really scared.

Size 10, please.

No one on Mom's train knew what happened yet.

When Dad got back to the pier, he saw a much bigger cloud of smoke than before, and he couldn't see the Towers anymore.

Dad didn't turn back. He skated and skated.

It was about twelve miles to the George Washington Bridge, the only bridge allowing pedestrian traffic into the city. By that point he found a pay phone that worked and was able to call my school as well as his parents in Puerto Rico.

He skated and skated. From the bridge to the park. From the park all the way home.

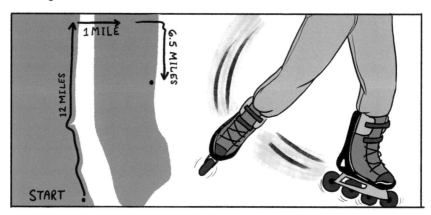

It was the only way to get home.

Mom must've been lucky to get the last train to Queens.

She told me you'd be here.

She's okay, right?

Today was scary for everyone.

We'll call her as soon as we get home.

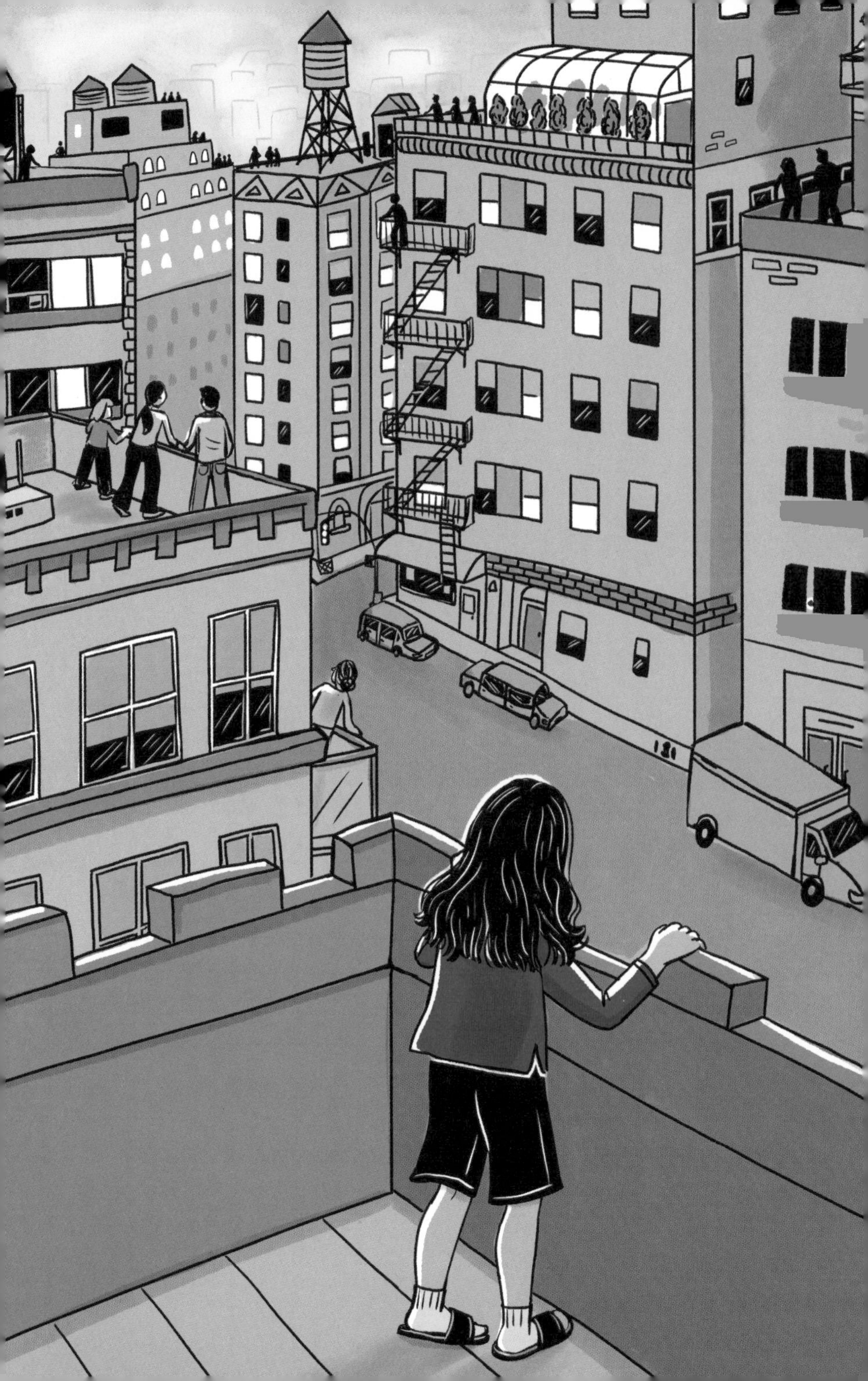

That night I went up to the roof and watched the sky. You could see and smell the smoke from up there. No one spoke a word.

September 19th, 2001

We've had to take everything extra slow because Mom is still sore from running down so many stairs. Her office building closed and people say it might collapse, too! There's sort of a quiet hush in the city now. It still feels like I am living in a bizarre dream. Strangers are making eye contact for the first time and it seems as though they just understand each other.

It feels like everyone in the city is connected by the same thoughts.

Almost everyone returned to school today. Luckily no one in our class lost a parent, but word traveled fast about the younger grades and why some of those kids were still absent from school. Everyone was whispering about terrorists and what they might look like.

When bad things happen, New Yorkers come together.

Our class, our school, city, and country all have experienced great loss...

...and we have to help those in need.

Let's split into groups of six.

Okay. Now I would like each group to come up with a list of people or ideas that they would like to pray for today.

Some of my classmates live downtown. For them it's like a war zone and everything is still closed. It was hard to talk about anything out loud because everyone had their own story inside them. Each story seems worse than the next.

Tonight I could hear planes taking off and landing. I don't think I've ever noticed them before. I sort of feel like I have no control over anything. I can't stop thinking about people dying.

I just want to disappear and come back. I want to come back to the normal life I knew and the Twin Towers that I visited with Dad all the time.

Dear Diary,

I know I haven't written in a while, but I haven't had a chance to focus on writing things down. Everyone in the city seems to be waiting for the next shoe to drop, between bomb scares and war talks. I remember when I first learned about the *Titanic* sinking. I thought about it for days and days, and it haunted me! This is different, though. It's different because it's in my home, and I didn't think anything like that could ever happen here. I can't stop thinking about everyone's families... I can't tell if the people around me are suffering.

I prayed today. To thank God, I suppose... And then I just cried and cried. I hid in my room with the music on so Mom couldn't hear me.

I know she's already trying to be strong for me and I don't want her to worry about me, too. In many ways I feel lucky... Our only direct loss was Dad's red bike. He built it from scratch twenty years ago and it had more than 10,000 miles on its speedometer. I guess it's a part of history now. I am so relieved he had that meeting in Jersey City.

Your grateful writer,
Alyssa

197

October 10th, 2001

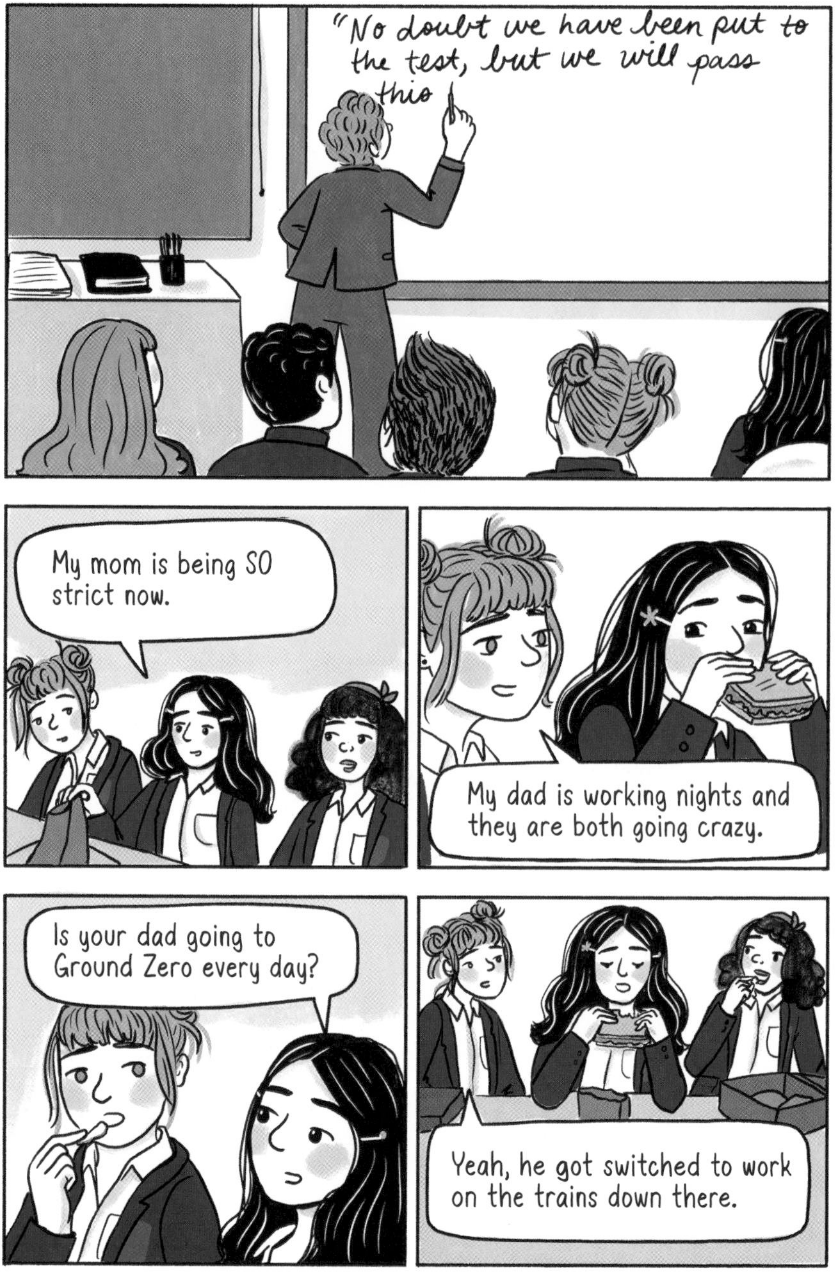
"No doubt we have been put to the test, but we will pass this
My mom is being SO strict now.
My dad is working nights and they are both going crazy.
Is your dad going to Ground Zero every day?
Yeah, he got switched to work on the trains down there.

BOO!

You nerds coming to the movies tonight?

I'm out.

Me, too...

Yooo, no one is allowed to do anything these days!

Mom has put forth some new laws. First, I have to take her cell phone everywhere so that I can call her at home and update her. If I don't pick up her call, I will be in big trouble.

I know we promised more freedom, but for now things will have to be different.

Second, I am socially limited to school, band practice, and Girl Scout meetings. That is it. For now I just have to go straight home to Dad's after any of these events. If something is happening on the weekend, I can only go if Mom or Dad can take me.

And don't spend your emergency money unless it's an EMERGENCY.

I got it...pizza is not an emergency...

I don't feel grounded, but it's not great, either. I sort of understand, though, and I don't want to see Mom worried like this anymore. It's scary when she can't control anything, either.

Sometimes I can't think of anything to say and sometimes she thinks I'm ungrateful, but I really do feel a little better after that.

October 16th, 2001

Sometimes I wonder how it's even possible to just continue life as normal! Our teachers either enjoy this torture or are trying to get us distracted from the city. Mom says it's good to put your energies into studies, but come on!

At least my friends and I are in the worry boat together. There are so many choices to weigh.

Everyone is obsessing over the future, the what-ifs, buts, and hows. There is so much pressure. I'm just trying to fit it all in my head.

October 25th, 2001

Today I had art class at the Met. I of course had to be dropped off and picked up by Dad. Once we got started I felt temporarily transported to another universe. Usually the Met is so crowded on the weekends, but the city is still pretty empty.

I had never used charcoal before.

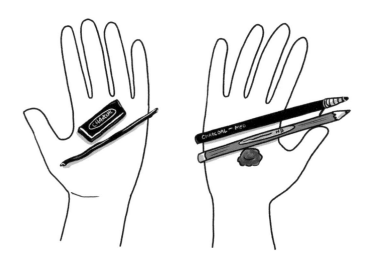

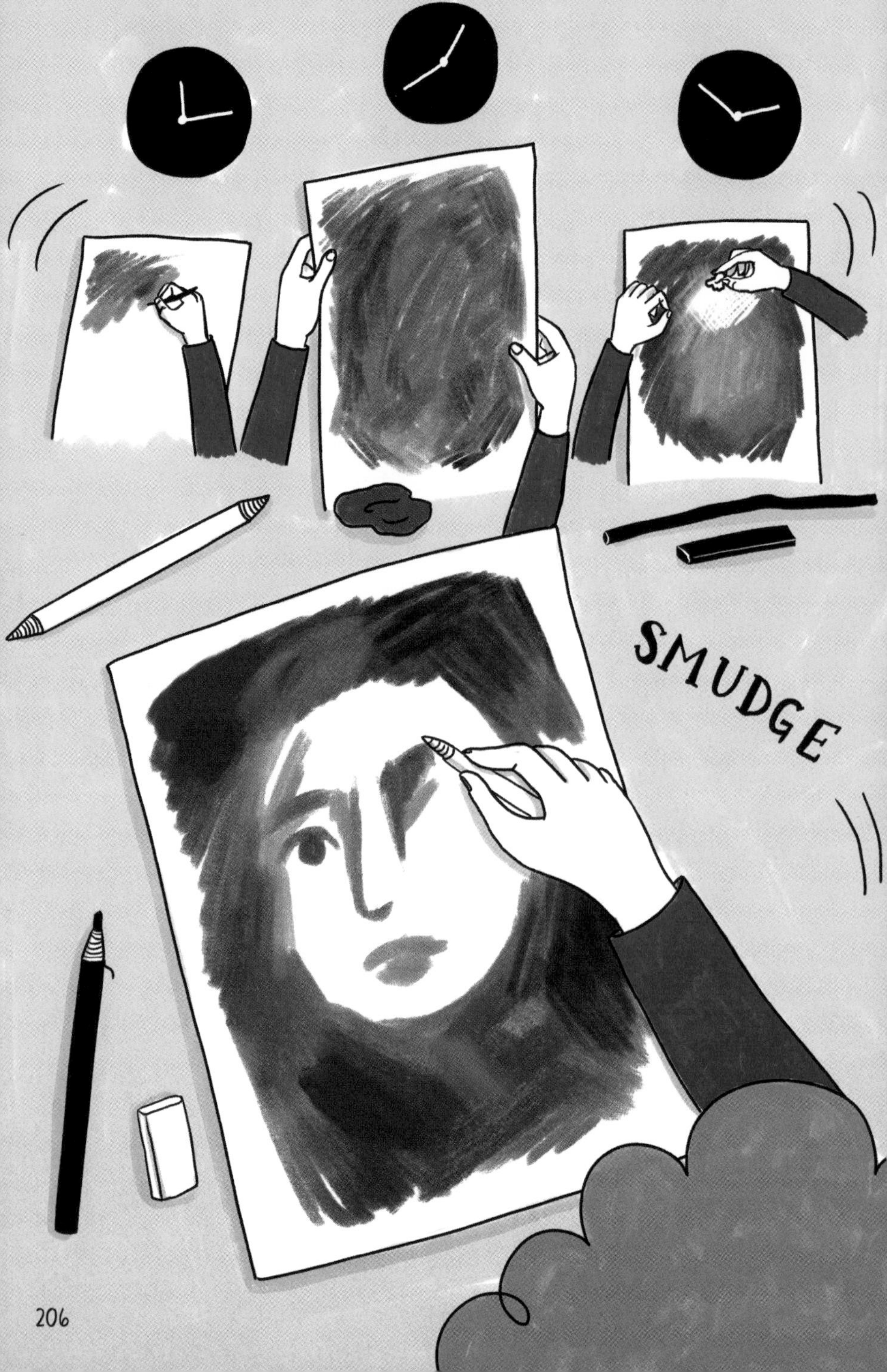
SMUDGE

SMOOSH

I couldn't believe when it was time to go. In those two hours the only thing on my mind was drawing. It seemed that time and sad feelings just disappeared for a little while.

November 3rd, 2001

Today we finally took the COOP exam, and to celebrate, Dad took me out to dinner.

I'm very proud of you and I'm sure you did well.

I hope so...

I know that there's been a lot going on lately and it's been especially hard to focus.

I've been feeling okay...

Good...good.

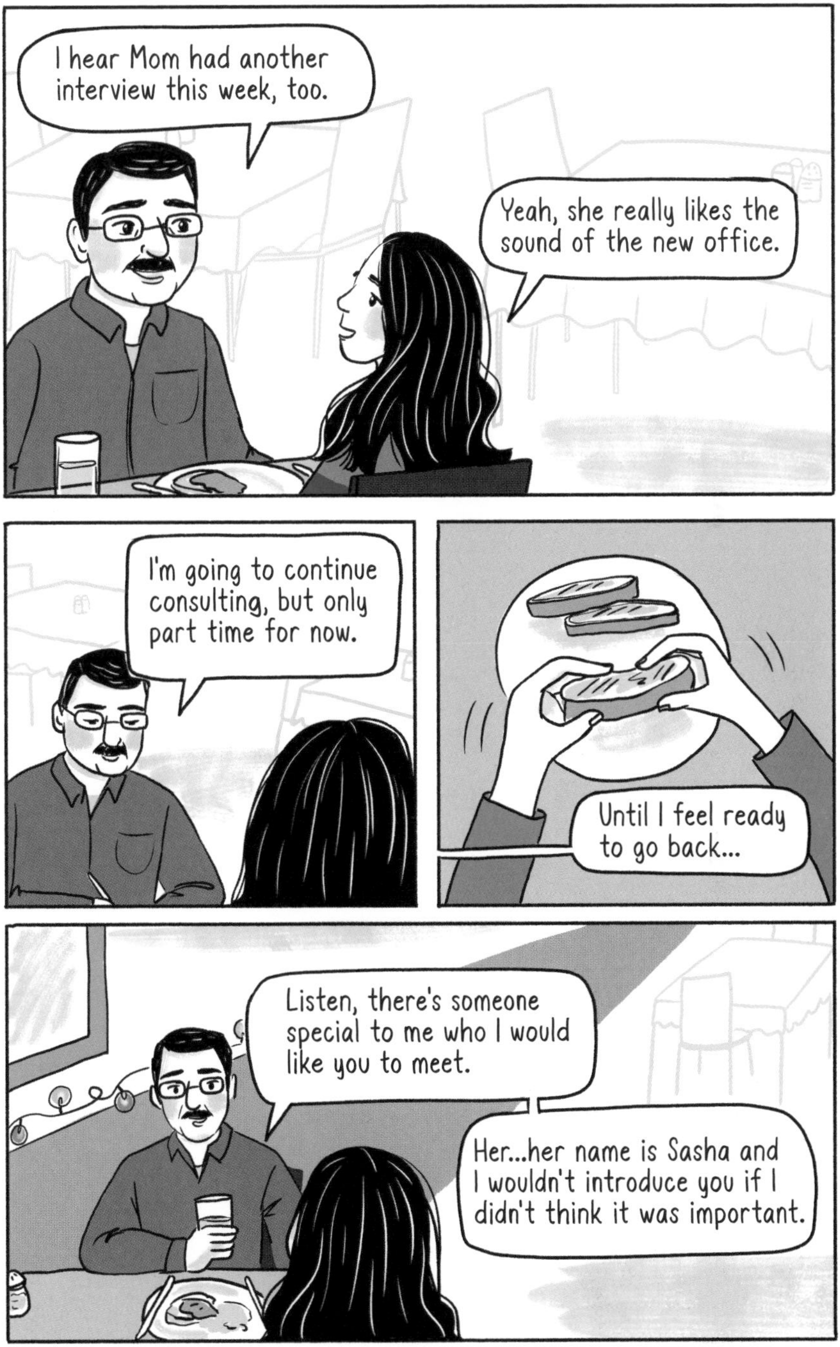
I hear Mom had another interview this week, too.
Yeah, she really likes the sound of the new office.
I'm going to continue consulting, but only part time for now.
Until I feel ready to go back...
Listen, there's someone special to me who I would like you to meet.
Her...her name is Sasha and I wouldn't introduce you if I didn't think it was important.

It was weird hearing my dad talk about his new girlfriend, but I also hadn't seen him that happy in a long time. It was really nice to see him that way.

November 6th, 2001

Mom got the job and starts this week! She is relieved that she won't ever have to go downtown again. Her commute will be similar to mine, unless I do end up going to high school in Queens. We won't find out until the new year. Who knows where I will be and what the future holds... When things can change in an instant, it's hard to accept it. I want to make the right decisions and prove my worth. I want to be brave.

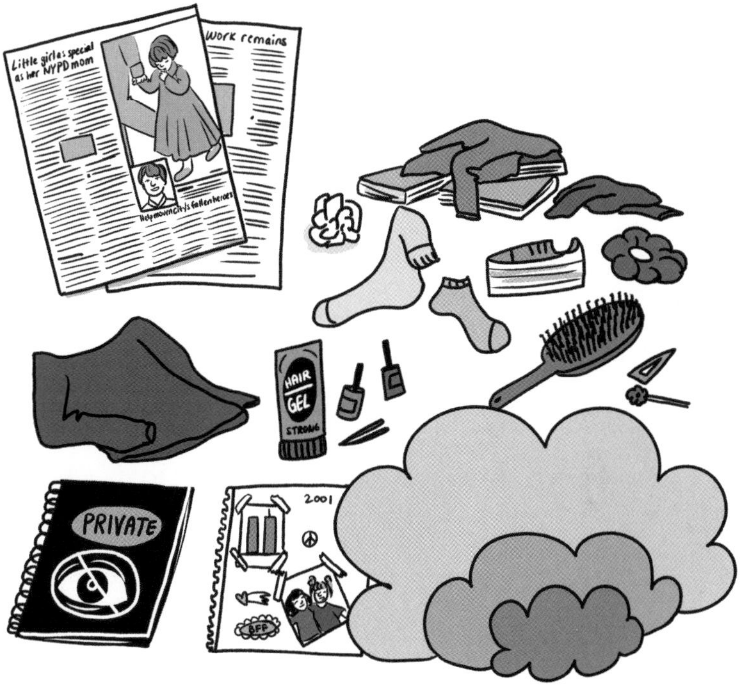
Little girl as special as her NYPD mom
Work remains
Help mourn City's fallen heroes
HAIR
GEL
STRONG
PRIVATE
2001
BFF

I decided to hit a slight refresh today. Between the weight of the world, COOP prep, and trying to look decent every day, I have been living in my own disaster zone room. Mom has been exceptionally patient about it, considering she usually pesters me about it NONSTOP.

When I was putting things away in the closet, I noticed the Alejandro rose was still there.

It reminded me of how happy I felt that day, so I decided to put it on my dresser where it was before. Back then everything was so much easier.

November 10th, 2001

Tomorrow is my thirteenth birthday! I'm excited but slightly conflicted, too. I feel selfish wanting to celebrate, but at the same time being a teenager is what I have wanted for SO LONG. Lucy's building has a meeting space, so it was my idea to have a small gathering there. I invited a bunch of people from school and my parents invited some of their friends, too. Now to prepare an outfit!

Well, it's official! 11/11!

It's been two months since the attacks and I hate that my birthday would be related in any way. I woke up with terrible cramps, but at least I am now a real-life teenager! It can only get better from here, I think. Mom has lifted the full fun ban and is allowing me some time after school and on weekends for hanging out, as long as I get home on time and call her.

November 15th, 2001

What a difference a year makes! Last year I was such a baby. I was SO obsessed with fitting in everywhere and having Alejandro like me back. ALL I wanted was to be free and for my parents to just leave me alone! A part of me still wants to belong at school, and be able to go out whenever I want, but there's just so much more to worry about on top of that now. I don't want to let anyone down, but more importantly, I don't want to let myself down.

We learned about "character" in Religion class. Your character is who you are when no one else is watching. I've been thinking so much about my character and I decided I'm going to try to be nicer to everyone because it's the right thing to do, not because I want them to be nice back. Dad said the world needs more kindness in a time like this.

Tomorrow my mom and I will have a mini Thanksgiving together. She invited a couple of friends who don't have families. My family isn't really "normal," but I'm okay with that. It's important to be there for people, especially for friends.

Lucy's family invited me over for turkey soup on Friday. Everyone has different traditions, I guess.

When I walked to pick up the pie we ordered, I noticed how festive everything looked. I was glad to see some things would always stay the same.

December 8th, 2001

Mom let me go ice-skating with everyone tonight! Dad had to drop me off and pick me up, which was SO embarrassing, but he met up with his GIRLFRIEND again so he didn't linger around the sidelines to torture me.

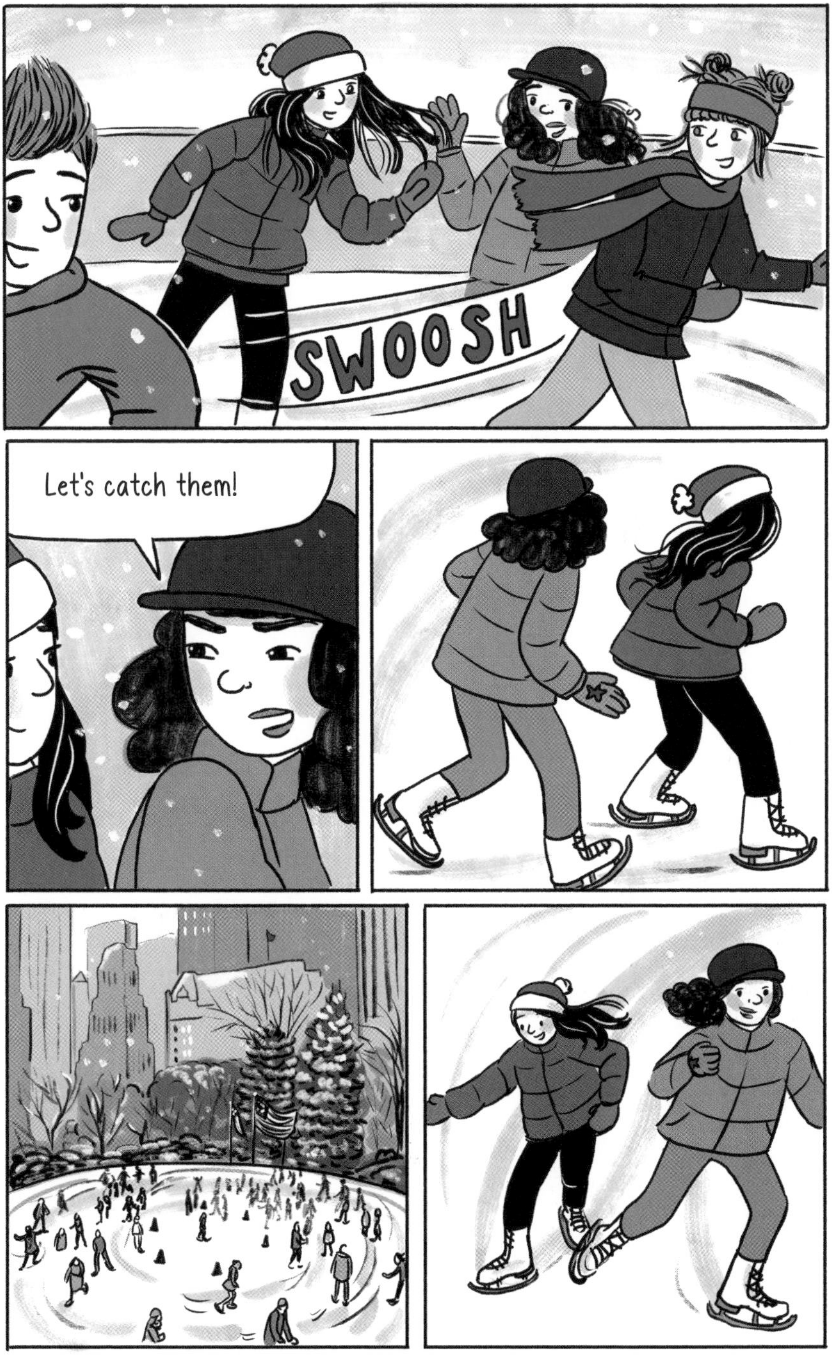
SWOOSH
Let's catch them!

OOF

We accidentally crashed into some cute boys on the way to warm up our hands. Whoops!

OT CHO

One by one we started singing along to the Christmas carols. I didn't even care how bad I sounded!

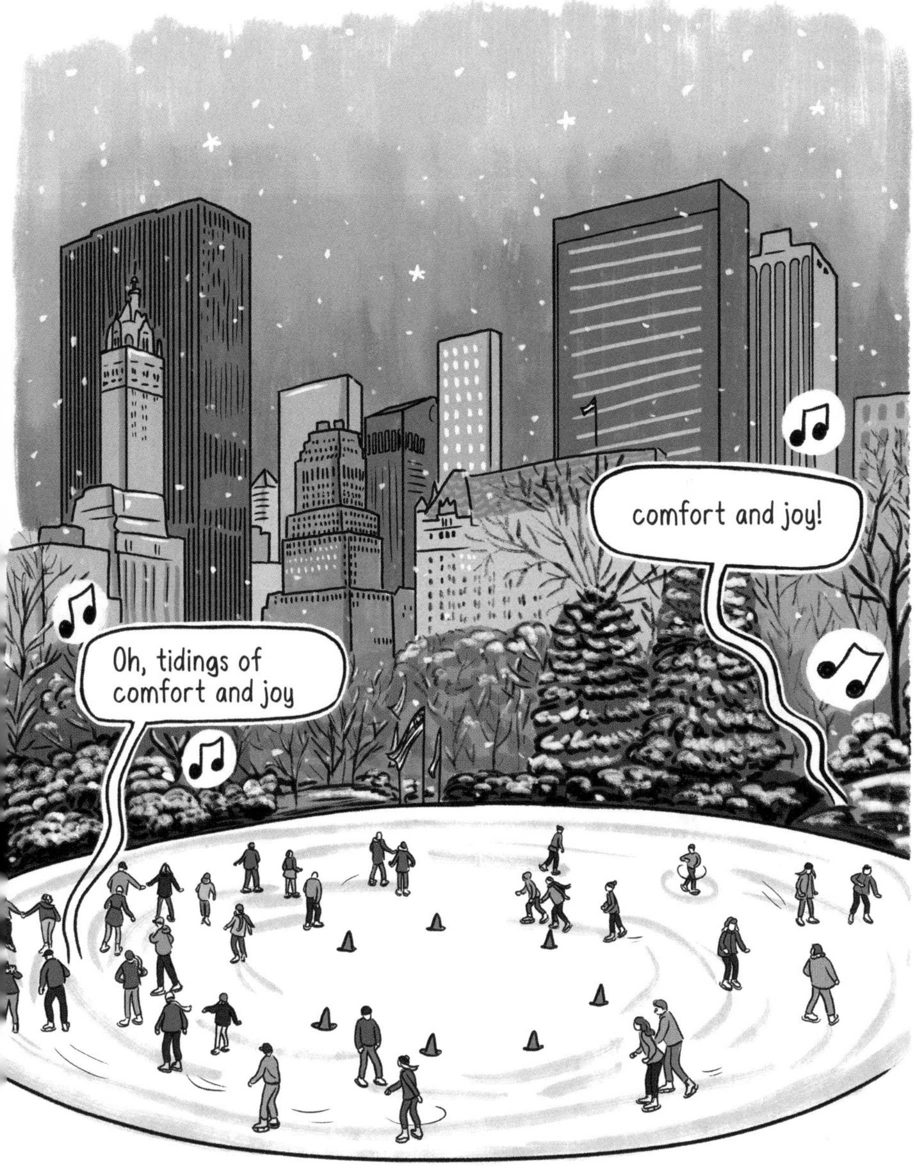
Oh, tidings of comfort and joy
comfort and joy!

December 16th, 2001

Sometimes everything feels completely normal. Everyday routines—going to school, doing homework, eating, going to bed. I don't even have time to think of how it might be different for other people on those days. And then other days it hits me...like today:

I can't believe Michelle is dating a high school guy.

I know...he's not even that cute.

Or nice...

haha

Yeah, they just hang out with that group because they think it's cool.

Totally.

PEACE ON EARTH

BLESS ★★★

WE WILL NEVER FORGET SEPT. 11 '01

This is a memorial for victims of 9-11-01. We hope that you take comfort here.

HER

We are with YOU.

PEACE

♥ NYC

How can anyone feel festive when those people aren't here anymore? I imagined my own family on the wall and it felt like my whole insides collapsed with the towers.

I tried not to think about it for too long, since I found I was just losing myself to their faces in my head and their stories flooding my mind. So I took my sketchbook and magazines out. It took a while to fade their faces into funky fashion and hairstyles, but once I started drawing, I had to fully dive into the proportions, lights, darks, and blending.

I was so deep under the layers
of each page and stroke that I
was able to calm myself down.

December 19th, 2001

Tonight felt a bit more Christmassy.

So I've decided to get another cell phone for us to use.

Really?!

It's still only for emergencies. I got a deal for free nights and weekends, though.

When do we start?!

After Christmas break.

Thanks, Mom.

Have you been doing okay lately?

Yeah. I'm okay.

There has been a lot of change recently and I'm proud of how you've handled it.

And with Dad having a girlfriend, too. How do you feel about that?

I actually think it's a good thing. Sasha is really nice and she's fun, too. I think Dad was really lonely. He seems a lot happier now... Are you okay with it?

Of course. What your father does is his business. I only care how it relates to you and if it bothers you at all.

No, it surprisingly doesn't bother me...

December 21st, 2001

I spent so long last night writing cards for everyone. It was our last day of school before the break and that meant we could dress up, too!

I was so happy to be with my friends and not thinking about high school or ANYTHING bad, but as I was waiting on the subway platform it also hit me that this was our last school Christmas together.

It feels more hopeful in the city now. There is a sense of strength in rebuilding and starting again. They say that our enemies would really defeat us if we stayed scared forever.

They say we have to show them that we are still strong and fight for what our country stands for. People around the country are asking what they can do to help in the war on terror...

The answer is to overcome evil with acts of goodness. I can do that. I want to do my part.

your hopeful writer,
Alyssa

Dear Diary,

New year, new me! In 2002 I want to be less shy, get better at drawing, and make the right choice for high school. Last year was crazy and I am ready for something better. I don't know what's going to happen, and I guess no one else knows, either. I don't know how to put my faith into it blind, but I will try. In Religion class they taught us to have faith in "God's plan for us." I hope I make the right choices. If He has a plan, I hope it's a good one.

GOODBYE 2001!

Lucy and I decided to make some changes for the new year.

We started out by trying some new hairstyles for 2002.

My cousin gave me her homemade hairspray, which makes your natural highlights come out. Technically it's not dye, so I think it's allowed.

I'm taking a leap of faith!

Your daring writer,
Alyssa

January 6th, 2002

Update on the spray bottle:

So I just spent a few days at Dad's trying to avoid my mom. He doesn't usually notice these things. I finally ran out of clothes and had to come back to my mom's.

My hair is now orange and I don't know what to do. It's definitely NOT the new look I wanted this year and I am going to be in so much trouble.

CODE ORANGE

LuCyGoOseY : AlyssasShoeZz

LuCyGoOsey: The Latin homework is killing me slowly!
AlyssasShoeZz: Umm, Lucy did you find out what was in that spray bottle?! Emergency. CODE ORANGE.
LuCyGoOsey: OMG, brb. I'll ask

January 8th, 2002

Well, Mom was horrified. I tried to deny it at first and just continue the evening like nothing happened, but there is no getting past Mom's All-Seeing Eye!

It looks even more orange in the sunlight. She says I have to grow it out to get rid of it and that I won't be allowed to dye my hair ever again. Luckily I'm not grounded! She says growing out this hair is punishment enough and a lesson well learned.

You're lucky your hair didn't all fall out! How could you do such a thing without knowing what was in the bottle?!

To be honest, I kind of like my hair being different...

January 10th, 2002

A simple task turned into quite the ordeal today. Mom always hates getting rid of the Christmas tree because the pine needles get everywhere. We live on the top floor of the walkup, which is lined in stinky old carpet.

You go downstairs and stand guard!

WHAT?!

ALL CLEAR!

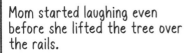

Mom started laughing even before she lifted the tree over the rails.

Here it comes!

HA HA

HA HA

SMACK

I haven't seen Mom laugh that hard in a while.

January 21st, 2002

This week everyone finds out what school they got into from the COOP exam. I have barely slept, thinking of my entire future. I don't want to disappoint everyone...and I definitely don't want to disappoint myself. There's so much pressure to make the right choice and I am terrified to make the wrong one.

1. Archbishop Molloy

2. The Mary Louis Academy

3. Dominican Academy

January 23rd, 2002

OMG. It just arrived. I got into the Mary Louis Academy (TMLA) and Dominican Academy! I got wait-listed for Molloy, though... Mom says that maybe it's meant to be and will make deciding easier. She doesn't seem too sad about it. Dad wasn't disappointed, either.

I got wait-listed...

Sweetie, I am very proud of you doing well on the exam and getting into the other schools.

It's very exciting!

Yeah, it's kind of crazy, huh?

I guess I am partially relieved to get into ANY school...but now I'll have to actually decide. What if I make the wrong choice?!

January 30th, 2002

I'm definitely going to Dominican—I've already accepted it!

Wow, that's so early! I didn't think we had to decide until March!

Michelle, Corrine, and a few others are going, too. We could all be together!

It's weird to imagine going to an all-girls school next year. If there are no boys there, how will I ever have a real boyfriend?

What if I have to start over completely? No one I know applied to TMLA... I want to decide what is best for me and not just where everyone else is going. I wish I had a crystal ball to just tell me what is right.

February 7th, 2002

I know it's weird that I still have the Alejandro rose. We don't really talk much, but we are still friends. I don't want to be a heartbreaker. Last year, when those dreams came true, it really was the best feeling. This year I don't have any Valentine's obsessions, but I am pretty excited for when Dad buys all of the chocolate on sale after.

February 15th, 2002

Tonight we had a family meeting. Usually when both of my parents are with me, it's for a school function or my birthday. I'm glad they are good friends because it would be much harder if they weren't.

Well, we will ultimately let you decide. There is something about TMLA, though. It would be nice for you to be more involved outdoors and in clubs.

I was very impressed with the facilities, and I agree that it would be great for you to join a sports team.

I don't know how to play ANY sports.

Well, you can learn! And going to school in Queens means you'll make new friends closer to home.

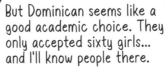
And it's more affordable...

But Dominican seems like a good academic choice. They only accepted sixty girls... and I'll know people there.

Yes, it is an excellent school.

But it is very small... and TMLA has an art cottage.

Yes, I know I am biased, but I can really see you there in that art cottage.

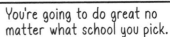
You're going to do great no matter what school you pick.

Right now I can't sleep because I am going back and forth. Dominican seems like the safe and obvious choice, but TMLA feels more like my destiny. If I'm going to be an artist one day, I probably need to go somewhere that can help me get there.

With Mom working overtime and Dad still only consulting these days I think I should go to the more affordable school, too.

I will have to start my whole life over if I choose that school. Maybe that's why it feels right. I just have a gut feeling that I belong there and can be whatever I want to be.

It is decided. I'm going to be a TMLA student in Queens.

Your late-night thinker,
Alyssa

February 23rd, 2002

Today we had our annual Coldest Day Ice Cream Eating Outing followed by some studying. It's crazy that we still have to take tests when we are all pretty much decided on schools, but there is no choice, of course.

Naturally, we got a little distracted at Lucy's place.

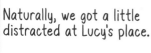

Oh, my god, I have a third eye.

At least your hair isn't orange.

HA HA HA HA HA

I usually put toothpaste on my zits. It totally works overnight.

I do, too! And my dad told me to put warm compresses on them.

TEEN

So we are all going to different schools next year...

It's going to be so weird.

At least you guys will know people at your school. I won't know anyone...

Well, you'll come hang out with us still!

Yeah, of course. And I'll always have to come see my dad so I'll have more excuses to come into the city now.

And we can come to Queens!

HA HA HA

March 11th, 2002

Today was the six-month anniversary. We wrote special prayers at school and they are still floating around in my head.

I will remember all of the firemen who ran up the WTC stairs—risking their lives to save others.

I will remember all of the volunteers who gave the workers at the site hope and encouragement.

I will remember the construction workers, who fought back every tear trying to find their friends.

I will remember the heroes on the planes, all different ages and cultures.

I will remember the American flag outside every window, billowing in the wind.

I will remember the WTC, tall and beautiful.

I will remember my strong country, and how we made it through.

Everyone in the city is debating whether to rebuild the Towers or leave it as a memorial site. Some say rebuilding will make our city strong again. Others say it will dishonor the people who are buried there. But if we don't rebuild, aren't we admitting defeat?

I'm not sure what the right thing is, but tonight they lit two spotlights in their place to shine into the sky for everyone to see. It reminds me of two infinite souls reaching up to the sky. We all just want to yell to the world that we are all people with the same morals and our gods all want us to live in peace, so how come we can't?

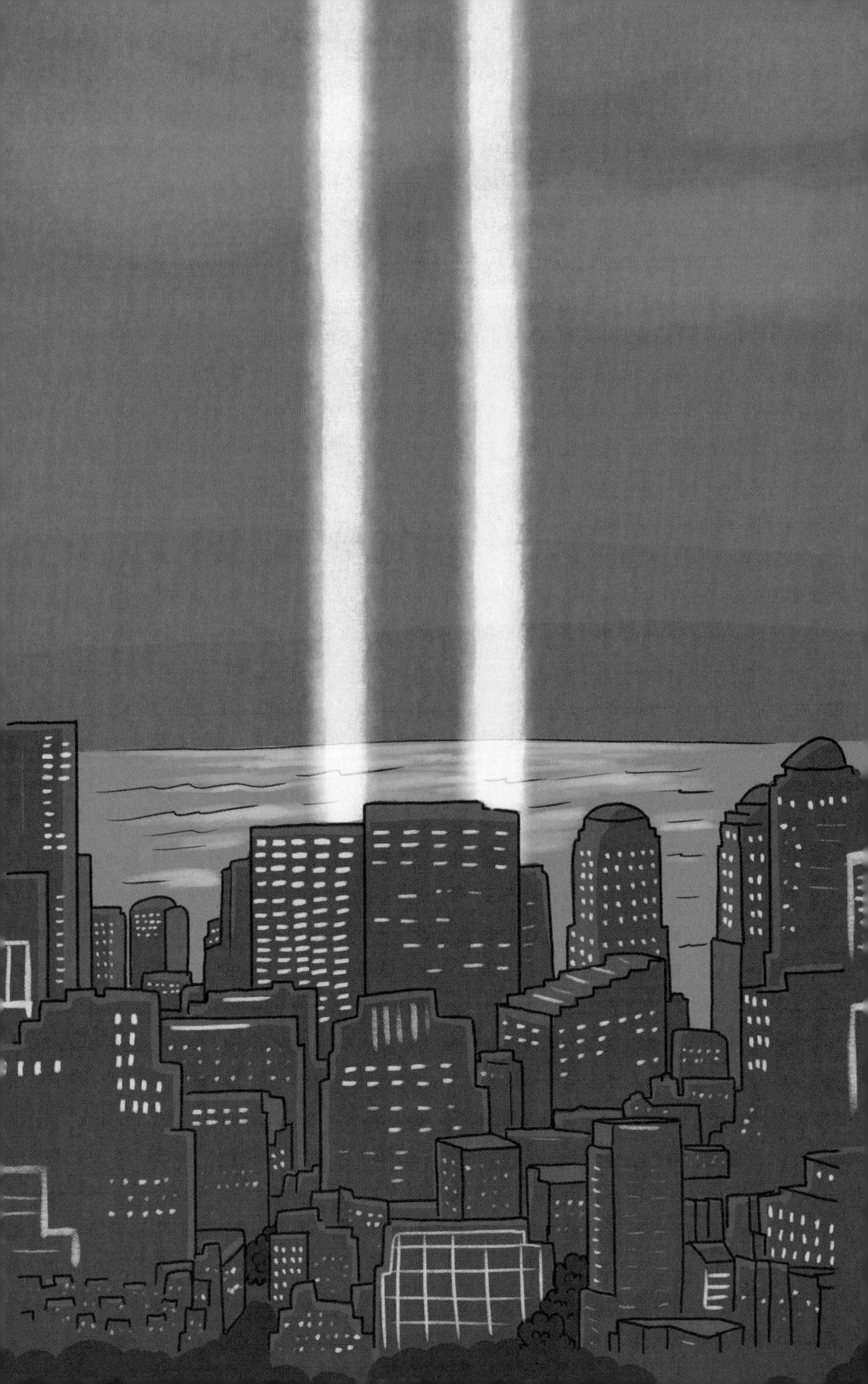

March 21st, 2002

Even after the big high school decision was made, I am still the same old studying-forever Alyssa. Some things never change, I guess.

LATIN VOCAB:

ROMAN HISTORY:

GODS & GODDESSES

STUFF TO KNOW

JUPITER

GOD of good HAIR DAYS

Minerva

Goddess of Wise SHOES

April 7th, 2002

I spent today with Dad and his girlfriend, Sasha. Usually Sundays are when we go biking. He's been a bit off lately and not biking as much. Biking is his whole world, so I knew it was strange.

Very funny. No, sweetie, I am just exercising a bit less these days and taking a break. I've been on a new medication for a few weeks and it's just one of the side effects.

Why do you have to take it?

It's not a big deal. I'm just having an issue with my liver. Things will be back to normal soon.

Well, good, because next month is the Five Boro Bike Tour. We can't miss that!

NUDGE NUDGE

Never!

Who's hungry? I want to take you guys to my favorite Puerto Rican restaurant!

ME!

DELI-GROCERY

DELI-GROCERY

ATM

COMIDAS

It's just a few more blocks! They have the best mofongo! You'll love it.

Julia de Burgos
1914 – 1953

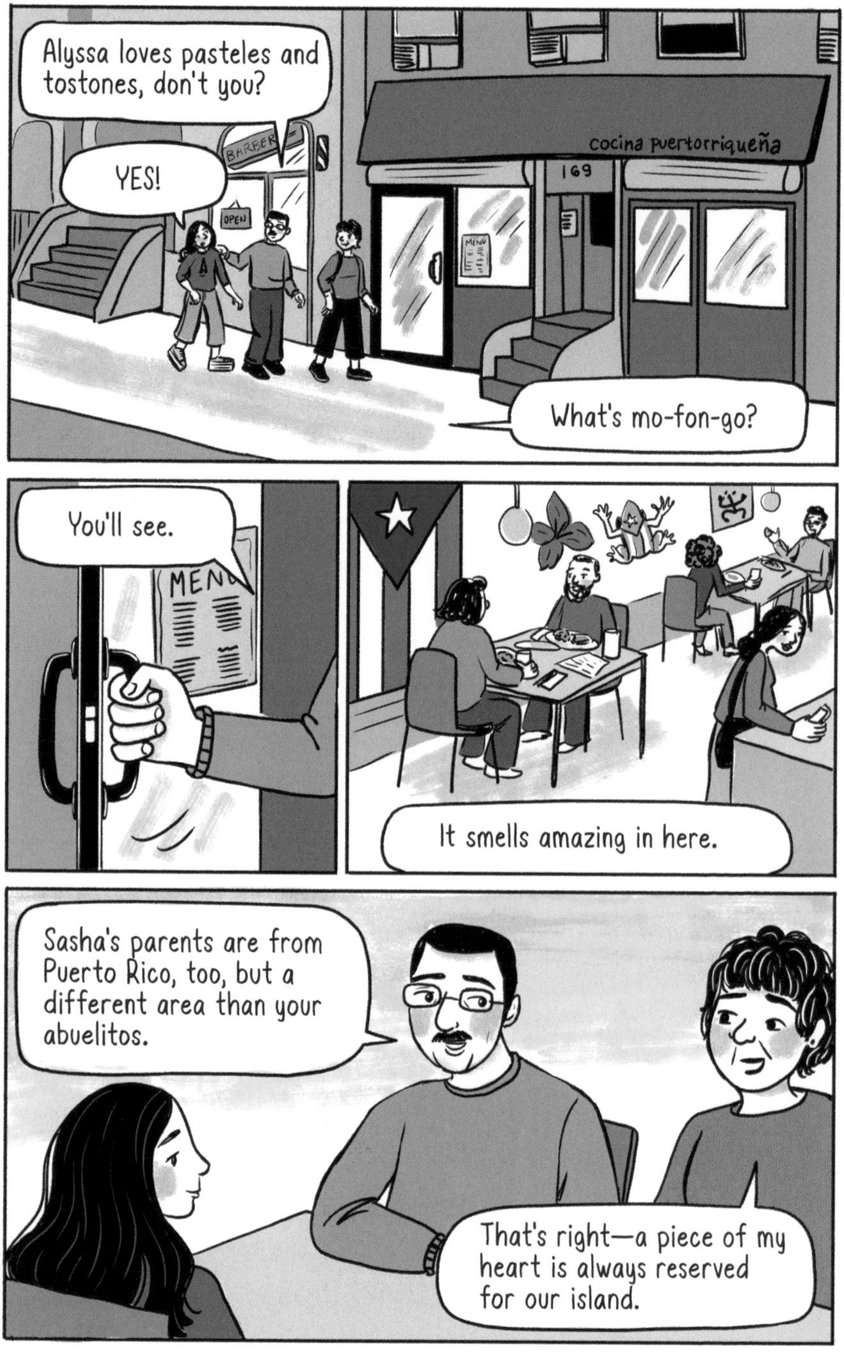
Alyssa loves pasteles and tostones, don't you?
YES!
BARBER
OPEN
cocina puertorriqueña
169
MENU
What's mo-fon-go?
You'll see.
MENU
It smells amazing in here.
Sasha's parents are from Puerto Rico, too, but a different area than your abuelitos.
That's right—a piece of my heart is always reserved for our island.

DAD. We have to go to Puerto Rico again as soon as possible and eat more of this.

MOFONGO ↗
♥

Yes, we certainly do. Grandma always goes out of her way to stuff us with food when we go visit. She'd be very happy to see you.

TAINO

As I ate all of the tasty dishes, I realized that no one can tell me who I am. I am Puerto Rican! Being there with Dad and Sasha made it seem like it just comes from the heart.

♥ your ♥
mofongo-loving
writer,
Alyssa

April 15th, 2002

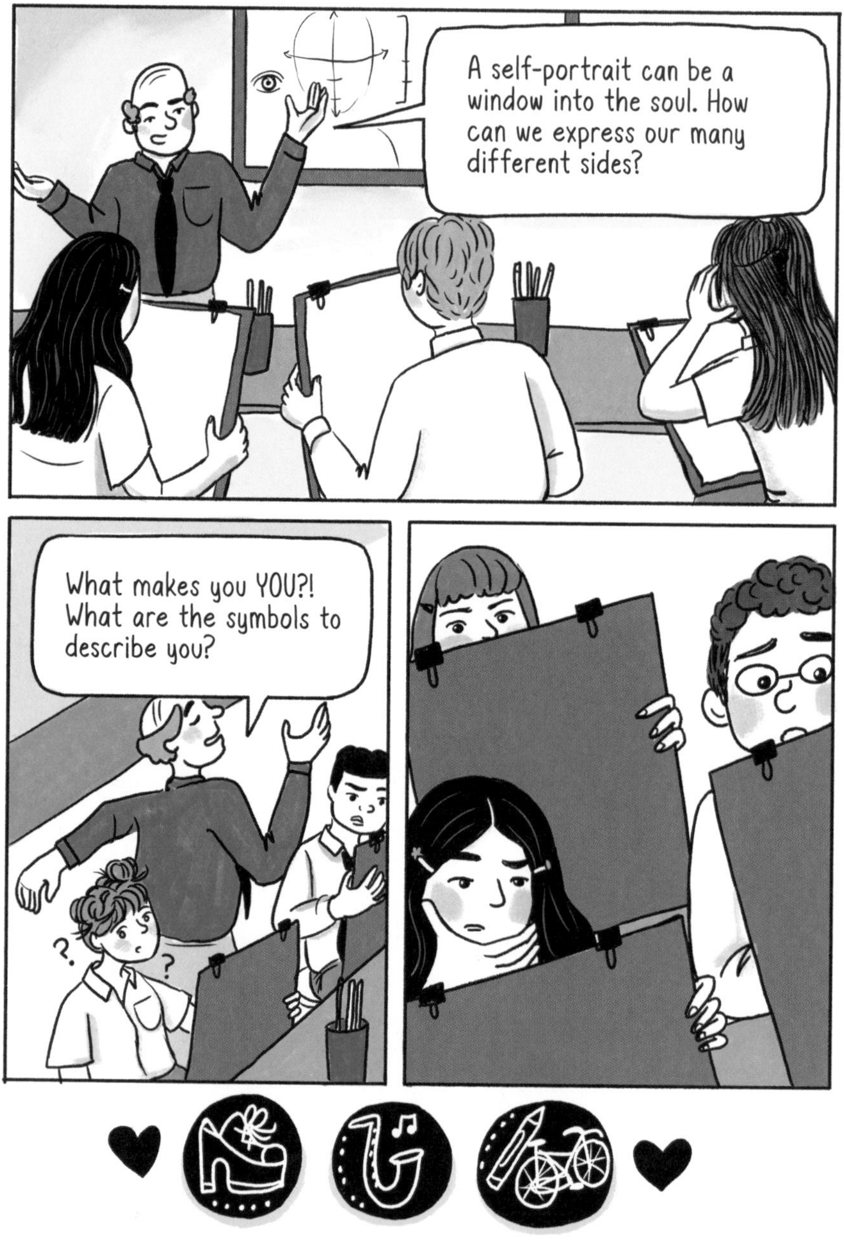

A self-portrait can be a window into the soul. How can we express our many different sides?
What makes you YOU?! What are the symbols to describe you?
?
?

You straight up look like a crackhead.

Whatever, dude, let's see yours.

I can't draw if my life depended on it.

C'mon, just show us. You're our only hope!

I'm still not done.

Usually my face burns up when there is attention on me, but this time was different. It felt really good to be noticed for my drawings. Sometimes it feels like everyone is smarter, sportier, and more popular than me...but today it felt like I was special, too.

your artistic writer,
alyssa

April 23rd, 2002

Sometimes I wish there was a hole to send me back to another time. In the olden days I probably would've already been married and spending my days cross-stitching by the fire. I wonder if they would've had more or less things to care so much about in those times. I guess no matter what time you come from, your family always matters.

What do you mean?

Well, with there being little work at the moment and my liver medication, it seems like a good time to focus on health and family.

But what does that mean?

It just means we will get to spend more time together. I'll start looking for work again in a couple of months. I will be done with this treatment by then, too, and back to my normal speed.

But you're going to be okay, right?

Of course. Sometimes we just need to take a step back and focus on what matters.

I didnt want Dad to think I was worrying about him or upset, so I held it all in and waited until I got to Mom's tonight to freak out. It just feels like as soon as I hit the teenage world, it hit me back, HARD. Mom reassured me that Dad actually is fine. However, it still seems as though change can happen in the blink of an eye and I can't catch up to it.

April 30th, 2002

It was the end of an era! The LAST band practice before the LAST concert.

The last of something usually means a first of something is coming soon after. I'm pretty nervous for what's coming next. I will NOT miss carrying my saxophone halfway across the world to get to school. My mom definitely won't miss me practicing the saxophone at home. I also won't miss Dad embarrassing me at concerts.

May 5th, 2002

Today was a cool, clear, crisp spring day. A part of me was happy, but it also reminded me of the Towers again. It was such a clear, crisp day then, too. I never thought that beautiful weather could make me so sad.

Still, every time I hear a helicopter, my heart skips a beat and I feel like I felt that day. In those moments it feels like the whole world is useless if peace can't be real.

May 10th, 2002

The Five Boro Bike Tour is when the whole city vibrates with energy. Dad and I do the forty-plus-mile ride every year together. When I was little he towed me behind him, but this year I'm ready to do it on my own. Even though his red bike is gone forever, today Dad decided to use his silver bike, which he takes out for special occasions or racing. Today everyone's wheels on the pavement moved together and it felt like we were all united as a city.

This year Dad brought Sasha, too.

It's different having her around, too, but I'm just glad Dad's back on a bike again! When he's on a bike, it's like the world is silent around him. That's sort of how I feel when I'm drawing, like I can tune the dial to my own station where nothing else is important.

We passed Ground Zero, which was blocked off with diggers.

Sometimes we had to take breaks.

Other times it was really hard, and we had to pedal through to make it,

but everyone else is there with you in the same struggle.

When we got to the end and finally made it there after using every muscle we're made of, the wave of pride hit us. I know Dad felt it, too. With almost 30,000 people riding this year, it felt like we were a part of something truly grand.

May 19th, 2002

Time is just going by so fast, as if I've suddenly woken up from a giant haze. In these eight years we've grown up so much and faced more than we ever imagined possible. Some moments I won't miss or want to repeat, but I'll still remember them, too, as part of the experience, I guess. It feels like everything we've been through at school has just glued us together and everyone's true colors came out.

I've been thinking a lot about life after graduation. I wonder what will happen to my friendships.

Mom says that to have a good friend, you need to be a good friend. It will be even harder when we won't see each other every day. They don't blame me for choosing a school far away from them or anything like that, but it was still a choice. I love them like family, and obviously I will miss them...but I also feel that good things are ahead of me. It's just a gut feeling and I want to explore what else is out there.

Going to a different school will lead to so many things! Who knows who I'll meet there and what it will mean for my future. With everything being able to change so suddenly, it's kind of nice to control this one part of my destiny.

June 3rd, 2002

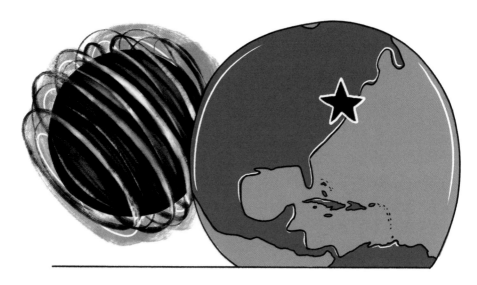

I used to think that Manhattan was the beginning and end of the world, and that it would always be that way with nothing setting it off course. It scares me sometimes to think that your whole life can suddenly change, that your friends might be different one day or that your family can be turned upside down. There are probably other girls just like me out there wondering what will happen next and if they are making the right choices.

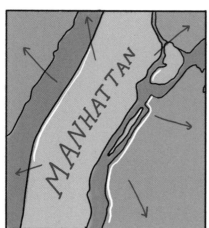

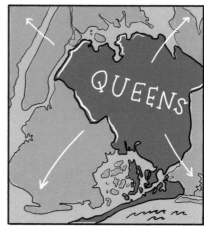

Graduation is just a few days away now. Starting over in a new school is going to be strange, without a doubt, but I can be whoever I want to be this time. I want to figure it out for me and not for anyone else. I am SO excited to go to school on a real campus like the high schools in the movies. Being able to take so many art classes is the icing on the cake! The only thing I am NOT looking forward to is the uniform shoes.

June 6th, 2002

Tomorrow I will be in the vast unknown space of my future. Some things I'll take with me, and other things I'll leave behind.

There will be decisions I'll have to choose on my own and some that will change in the blink of an eye...but either way, I think I'll be okay. I'm ready.

Your writer,
Alyssa

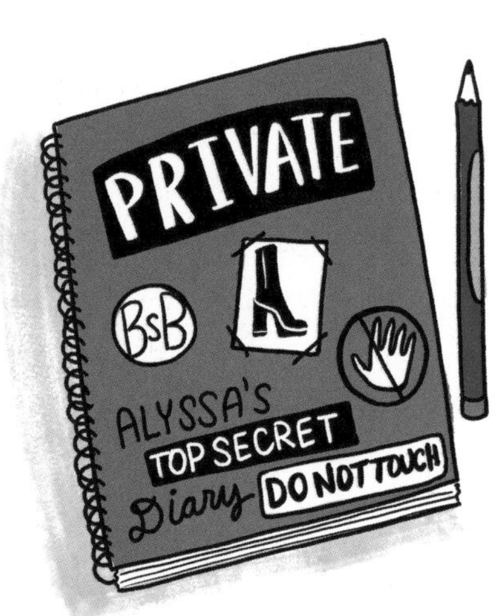
PRIVATE
BsB
ALYSSA'S
TOP SECRET
Diary
DO NOT TOUCH

AUTHOR'S NOTE

When I moved out of my mom's Queens apartment in my early twenties, I found my childhood diaries, which were so precious to me at the time they were written. As a painfully shy, insecure tween, I don't know what I would have done without them! I gradually started sharing some of the funnier entries with friends and family and soon realized that sharing them created a wider conversation about the woes of growing up. I recreated a few of my favorite diary moments in comic form and since then the idea has snowballed into this book.

Many of my real diaries

While I didn't become a shoe designer, I did major in Fashion Illustration at FIT in Manhattan. I realized that the core of what I loved was the drawing itself and not the leatherwork, stitching, and crafting of actual shoes. I have continued to work as an illustrator and art teacher ever since.

Most of this story is completely true. Many of the diary entries are exactly as I wrote them. Yes, I did shave off my eyebrows and dye my hair orange accidentally. My dad really did Rollerblade home that fateful day. Brian Littrell is still my favorite Backstreet Boy and Alejandro moved back to Colombia eventually. Some of the school characters are blended together, so I have changed all of their names. I'm still in touch with many of them.

My thirteen-year-old self could barely see ahead to high school, and was terrified of the unknown. She would never believe that thirteen years later she would move across the world to Australia on a leap of faith without ever having lived anywhere but New York City. This change would ultimately be the biggest of all!

It wasn't until I moved from New York to the other side of the world that I realized how essential the New Yorker side of this story was, and I began to weave that in. While I truly did keep a dedicated diary from ages eight to eighteen, I did not actually write about what happened on September 11, 2001, until ten years later. Everyone handles traumatic experiences differently, especially as a child. To explore that part of this story, I revisited that transitional time period with several of my classmates to piece it all together from our different points of view. In addition to this, a close friend of mine who attended a different NYC school generously lent me her special 9/11 diary with poems, reflections, and news articles that she saved during her coping process. She wrote in it that her intention as a thirteen-year-old was "to help kids in the future understand what it was like."

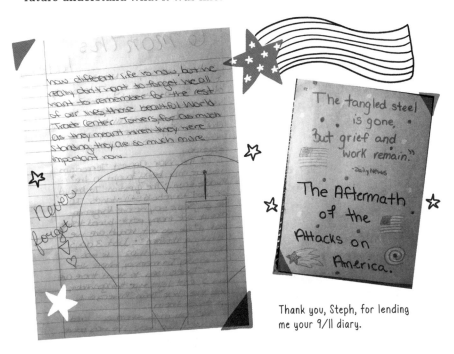

how different life is now, but we really don't want to forget. We all want to remember for the rest of our lives those beautiful World Trade Center Towers, for as much as they meant when they were standing, they are so much more important now.

never
forget

"The tangled steel is gone, But grief and work remain."
-Daily News

The Aftermath of the Attacks on America.

Thank you, Steph, for lending me your 9/11 diary.

Although my dad was lucky in September 2001, his health was slowly deteriorating. In hindsight, I included hints at what he was going through, which I didn't recognize as serious at the time. He passed away in July 2003, and my world was again changed forever.

DAD

Dad's red bike

MOM

John Orlando Bermudez
1950–2003

The Towers were in almost every photo album from my childhood.

In some ways, middle school life is very different all of these years later, whether in a big city or not. However, the feelings that come with middle school are universal and timeless. From self-exploration to painful embarrassment, everyone else is feeling it with you. Change can be scary, but sometimes it leads to something wonderful. I hope young readers will surprise themselves in the future with their own growth and bravery beyond their imagination!

Your grown-up writer,

Alyssa Bermudez

ACKNOWLEDGMENTS

This book would not have been possible without the support and encouragement of so many invaluable people.

Thank you, Claire and Lori at Painted Words, for pushing me forward to put this book out there. Thank you, Connie Hsu, for believing in the story I was trying to tell and much more. Thank you to the amazing team at Roaring Brook for making this dream come true!—Kirk Benshoff, Sunny Lee, Megan Abbate, and countless others working behind the scenes.

Big thanks go to my former classmates at Saint Ignatius who contributed awkward and heartfelt memories from that time. Thank you, Stephanie, for sharing your beautiful and honest 9/11 diaries with me. Thanks and hugs to my husband, friends, and family for applauding me and laughing with me along this journey.

I have so much gratitude toward my parents, for opening my eyes to the magic of art and writing as a child. My mom is the bravest person in the whole world, and I thank her for letting me share this book, which is just as much her story as it is mine. Thank you for being my cheerleader.

Lastly, I would like to thank my former eleven-to-thirteen-year-old self for choosing to write in a diary, never knowing it would be shared with the world twenty years later. How crazy is that?!

Photo credit: Max von Saurma

ALYSSA BERMUDEZ is a born and bred New Yorker now living down under in Australia. She studied illustration and animation at the Fashion Institute of Technology. After spending many years working for magazines, agencies, and schools as an art teacher, she moved across the world to Hobart, Tasmania, where she works as a freelance author and illustrator. Her illustrations can be found in many books including the Lucia the Luchadora series and the Amelia Chamelia series.

alyssabermudezart.com